# Revolutionary School Culture

## The 6 Principles of Unlocking Your School's Hidden Treasure

**Amen Rahh**

Published by Revolutionary Education Publishing
A Division of Revolutionary Education LLC
Paperback ISBN: 978-1-7361192-0-4
Ebook ISBN: 978-1-7361192-1-1

Cover Design by Alexis Moorer

"Informative and inspiring; real and refreshing, Amen Rahh has provided us with the definitive book on leadership. If you are a leader in search of a comprehensive work on how to create a revolution in education, search no more. Principal Rahh offers practical strategies, culturally responsive approaches, and revolutionary principles that every educator needs to take to heart if you believe in the potential and promise of our youth. A must read for those who have a no-excuses, no-nonsense mindset on getting schools right. Every educator needs this book." – *Dr. Tyrone C. Howard, Ph.D. Director, UCLA Center for the Transformation of Schools*

"There are far and few books out there where you feel the passion and drive of the author from page one. With the simple words, LET'S BOOM, Principal Rahh cements his message that all students deserve an experience at school that draws upon their culture, identity, and individuality. Not only does Rahh draw upon scholarly research, but he brings in his personal stories of building a revolutionary school that will inspire and offer a blueprint for others to follow. The simple steps he takes and lays out mixed with the real talk on social justice that is desperately needed in every school will leave you rejuvenated for your career and inspired to make positive change for your students." – *Adam Dovico, Principal, Author, Speaker, and Professor.*

"In *Revolutionary School Culture*, Principal Rahh delivers truth in a unique way that is both powerful and digestible. As our world continues to transition and adapt, we need leaders who are progressive about learning strategies that will help increase the self-efficacy of every child we will encounter. This book will allow you to expand your thought process as we continue to elevate in education." – *Michael Bonner, Teacher at the Ron Clark Academy, Author, Educational Consultant*

# DEDICATION

To my wife, children, family, and friends thank you for pushing me to continue my marathon.

To my school family at The U, we made history together.

To my students in Compton and Watts, never let them dictate who you are supposed to be.

To Nipsey Hussle, thank you for you inspiring me to be a better educator.

To that educator who is ready to take full control of their minds and spirit as they continue to fight for liberation through education...

Welcome to your revolution.

# Table of Contents

**CHAPTER 10:**

**Principle 5: Revolutionizing Your Data-Centered Culture** . . . .133

**CHAPTER 11:**

**Principle 6: Revolutionizing Teaching and Learning** . . . . . . . .143

**CHAPTER 12:**

**Revolutionizing Your Community** . . . . . . . . . . . . . . . . . . . . . .153

# Foreword

By Dr. Cynthia Gonzalez and Brandon "Stix" Bailey

A Revolution is only possible when it is centered on the wellness of a community.

I had the opportunity to meet Amen Rahh while we learned to be trainers of trainers for Restorative Practices. During this time, I had the opportunity to witness his passion for his work, specifically, the world of education. Not only was he a committed educator, but he understood what every great educator understands, that RELATIONSHIPS are the key to the promise of true revolutionary education. As luck would have it, I bumped into Amen during a district shut-down. I recognized him from our training. I was serving as a principal for a small high school in South Central that was undergoing a turnaround effort. The school was comprised mostly of male students of color. I knew that in order to help my school make the shift my students deserved, I would need to hire someone who could motivate, inspire, and cultivate the relationships necessary for change, and that person was Amen Rahh.

During his tenure at our school, he did not disappoint. He worked his revolutionary educator 'magic', making students feel seen and known, and increased their sense of belonging. He greeted students with unique handshakes, led events to build and sustain a school culture that would allow us to make the turn that we needed. It was no surprise to me that he was quickly offered a position, to not only lead his own school, but to build it from the ground up. He took this responsibility both with enthusiasm and care. His decision-making at every point of his journey kept students at the center. His mission was to create a school in Watts that students there deserved. See, Revolutions demand intention. Those who seek to make the changes they deem of value for our society must do so with tact and precision.

If you see yourself as a Revolutionary Educator, this book is for you. If you aren't sure if you see yourself as a Revolutionary Educator, but it is something you are striving for, this book is for you. If you know that something in your school needs to change in order to make it a space where every voice feels valued, seen, and heard, then this book is for you.

Leadership matters greatly. Charisma, when people have it, can be a great ignition for change. But to be a Revolutionary Educator requires much more than charisma. It demands a deep commitment to values and principles that seek to improve the lives of others through relationship building, setting high expectations, and building the structures necessary for change. This book will guide you through practices in which you can engage, to make revolutionary education a reality at your school. This book matters because we have hundreds of schools that require Revolutionary Educators.

In the words of Amen Rahh, "Let's BOOM!"

In this book, you will experience the true meaning of what revolutionary education means. I'm sure we've heard this before, that a principal should be your pal. Most principals have forgotten about that unwritten rule. Relationships drive our success, and having them is the key factor in how we succeed in this challenging and ever-changing nation. Amen Rahh exemplifies that pal; Rahh exemplifies the phrase, *'Building Relationships'*. To most, getting a pie in the face for not knowing a student's name is unorthodox and a waste of time, but to Rahh, it's relationship-building and culture development.

In this book, it will also be revealed that the term 'system' and 'oppression' go hand-and-hand. The education system has failed, yet we still enforce old models that mimic prison culture on our children. We discovered that the curriculum currently encourages our students to be mediocre, yet the limits that can be obtained are ignored to induce in the minds of our young kings and queens. But, how dare you teach a young human being in school that they can be great. That's not a principal's job. A principal, a.k.a. the 'warden', is to enforce policy and manage law of the system they protect. Rahh, on the other hand, begs to differ. Understand that systematic means automatic, and Rahh is no robot. Furthermore, non-traditional might be his favorite approach.

More importantly, in this book, you might run across topics like macroeconomics and economic justice. Now, these topics are blasphemous coming out of a principal's mouth. Principals should be focused on recruitment, attendance, and test scores so they don't have time to educate citizens on macroeconomics. I laugh in the face of normality and the curriculums put in place by slaveholders who knew exactly what they were crafting in their laboratory, called the Board of Education. They had no clue that a child born in Compton, named Amen Rahh, would challenge everyone and everything known as the 'system'.

Thank you to our educator ancestors, Fanny Jackson Coppin, Kelly Miller, and Mary McLeod Bethune.

# Introduction

*"We can't teach what we don't know, and we can't lead where we can't go."*
*(Malcolm X)*

It's time for a revolution. Now, repeat after me, "I AM THE REVOLUTION."

This isn't something you would commonly hear in the world of education. But with the way things are going now, I think this statement makes a powerful impact. As educators, it's time for us to start making real changes. These changes are meant to provide equal opportunities to all students—not just the same selection of students who have been enjoying more privileges and opportunities than others.

Although we have all grown accustomed to the current state of our educational system, this doesn't mean that we cannot improve it. No matter how perfect something may seem, there is always a way to make it better. And when it comes to education, things are far from perfect. This means that there is a lot of room for positive change. As an educator, a leader, or someone who wants to inspire and motivate others, you will learn everything you need to know in this book to start your own revolution. In the words of "The Community," you need to inspire or retire!

In this book, you will discover concepts like revolutionary leadership, strategies to initiate transformation, organizational culture, and specific steps for how you can start making a change for the better. If you have always wanted to initiate change in your school or educational system but you don't know where to start, you are about to embark on a journey, during which you will learn valuable information that will help you and your team to achieve your goals.

But, before we start this transformative journey of yours, let me tell you more about myself to give you an idea of how this book came to be and why I decided to write it.

I am proud to say that I was born and raised in the wonderful city of Compton, California, by my mother, Abwakiya Rahh, and my father, The Legendary Professor, Amen Rahh. I was the youngest of six children. My father, Professor Amen Rahh, was a Councilman in Compton and a School Board Trustee. Now, he is a retired Professor from Compton Community College and California State University of Long Beach. My father is known for establishing the Black Studies program at The University in the early 1970s. Much of my inspiration comes from my father and the amazing things he has accomplished in his life. I remember my father telling me, "You may not feel like you are at war, but you are in a war." When I was younger, I didn't fully understand what this meant. But now I know that he was referring to the struggle of fighting oppression and injustices as a constant war. Therefore, I must always be aware of the issues that are taking place around me. This awareness has carried me to places I never thought I would reach.

I received my Associate's Degree from Compton Community College, and my Bachelors of Arts Degree in Black Studies from Cal State University Dominguez Hills. Prior to receiving both of these degrees, I was an aspiring rapper and football player. I even had a rap name, which was "Solo." But shortly after I gave up on my rap career, I had a devastating knee injury, which shattered both of those dreams. Still, I pressed on. I moved forward with my education and strove to "pull myself up by the bootstraps." I also happen to be a certified trainer of trainers in Restorative Justice by the Institute of Restorative Practices (IIRP). My long, fulfilling, and still continuing professional career began when I was hired as a Special Education

Assistant. Through the years, I have grown, evolved, and risen through challenges to become who I am today.

My name is Amen Mandela Rahh and I am a Revolutionary Principal.

This title of this book came from how I founded and built the University Pathways Public Service Academy. More famously known as "The U", this is one of the most well-known urban public schools in South Central Los Angeles. Through the years, I had managed to set myself apart in the classroom and as a leader of the school. Back when I was a middle school teacher in Watts, California, I was chosen as the "turnaround teacher." Ultimately, this helped me obtain the position as Dean of Student Success at the young age of 24. At the age of 29, I had founded one of the most highly regarded schools by parents and students in the Los Angeles area.

Currently, I am not just known as "Principal Rahh", a title that I hold in high regard. I live with my beautiful wife, Danielle Rahh, and our equally beautiful daughter, Journee. Aside from being a principal, I also happen to be a speaker who focuses on transforming the way schools serve their at-hope students here in America. I am a published author of a chapter I wrote in the book entitled, "Restorative Practices Meets Social Justice." Over the years, I have also received many professional, community, and educational awards. But before I go on, let me share an interesting fact with you. Have you read the book, *The Alchemist* by Paulo Coelho? If you haven't read it yet, I highly recommend it. I got a lot of inspiration from this book, as it is about a man named Santiago who went on an adventure to find his life's purpose. In fact, I added the term, "Hidden Treasure" in this book's title to pay respect to this life-altering book, as it changed my life. In turn, I hope *Revolutionary School Culture* will change yours as well.

I was chosen to be the Founding Principal to revolutionize the educational experience for my community. As a leader, I can say that

I am mission-driven, as I seek to empower each individual student to be better than the best version of themselves. My school was founded in 2018, and in our second year, it was already considered a model school by the state of California for building a Restorative Community, as well as establishing a school-wide system to improve student achievement–another thing of which I am extremely proud.

As you can see, I already have extensive knowledge and experience in the world of education, but I am far from being done. As a Revolutionary Principal, I will always strive to enlighten others and inspire people like you who want to learn how to change your existing educational environments. After reading this book, I promise you that you will have a more enlightened perspective on how you can start making the change you have always wanted to initiate in your school. Not only that, but you will also be equipped with all the effective and practical strategies you need to start taking action! If you are ready to learn the wealth of information contained within the pages of *Revolutionary School Culture*, then let us start this journey together. Turn the page and LET'S BOOM.

# Chapter 1:

# We Need a Revolution: Revolutionary vs Evolutionary

*"You cannot buy the revolution. You cannot make the revolution. You can only be the revolution. It is in your spirit, or it is nowhere." (Le Guin, 1974)*

Ever since I could remember, I always aspired to become a leader. Back when I was still starting out, my mentor was a school principal who explained the most important things I should do when I get my time as a principal. During my first year, I should focus on observing those around me and building relationships. During my second year, I should start implementing the ideas I have. When I reach year three, I should focus on making improvements—then I would have to wait for about three more years to see any difference. Then he explained that the typical "shelf-life" of a principal at a school is three years.

So what was I supposed to do?

Now, try to imagine yourself as a new principal at a school. Knowing that your ideas, plans, and initiatives will only start to make an impact in your third year, but, paradoxically, your third year is when you will probably either move to another school, be released for not making improvements to the school, or get promoted.

In such a situation, you might feel discouraged, but this isn't the point I want to make. The point here is that the three-year period of evolution is natural, and it will happen no matter what, as long as you initiate it. But the good news is that there are practical systems that you can implement as the leader of your school that will make an immediate impact. These are the things you should focus on too, but you can only do these things if you truly understand why the education system in America needs to change, and how students are not being properly served by the current structure. To let your revolution begin... let's BOOM!

## The Current State of the US Educational System

An abundance of research and several studies have concluded that the social class of students is a significant predictor of their success in education (Garcia & Weiss, 2017). In fact, some argue that this might be the most significant predictor. Salient research is out there about how when young children start their educational journey from one of the lower social classes, they tend to experience gaps in their performance. Unfortunately, this narrative has caused educators to lower their expectations and have many preconceived notions, and judgments about the a.k.a. "urban and culturally-diverse" schools and districts that have Black and Latinx students. Sadly, many educators have used these grim statistics to form negative ideas about "those students" or "these kids" in the current education system in the US.

But such statistics aren't new.

According to the National Center for Education Statistics, in 2014, the graduation rate for white high school students was 87%, but only 73% for black students. In the same year, test scores had shown a similar gap. But academic performance isn't the only problem. Compared to white students, there is a higher likelihood of black students to be either expelled or suspended from school. Conversely, there is a smaller likelihood of black students getting into gifted programs compared to white students—this isn't by accident. As I mentioned before, these negative ideas have impacted and reinforced a systematic issue of schools having lower expectations when it comes to Black students.

The aforementioned are just some examples of the devastating state our current educational system is in right now. And if you just accept this state, equality will never exist.

## What is an Anti-Racist School?

Becoming an Anti-Racist School is a fight against institutional racism. Institutional racism refers to a society's systematic distribution of opportunities, power, and resources to the benefit of white people, while excluding people of color. This concept is characterized by racial biases and bigotry. It exists in societies and institutions where the main focus is on a culture of assimilation and white supremacy. Many feel that institutional racism isn't as rampant now as it was in the past; however, we can still see it clearly in several situations. Here are some examples:

## *Restrictive Covenants in Housing Contracts*

Access to housing impacts the culture of achievement for students. Although racial covenants—statements that say that properties can only be conveyed, leased, or rented to white people—have been rendered illegal, you will still find creative techniques used in language in deeds and contracts all over America. This makes it extremely difficult for people of color to find homes, loans, and affordable housing, especially within a system of banking that is primarily populated with conditions that still practice racism. I repeat, this is an access issue.

## *Redlining in Bank Lending*

*"They don't teach us how to sell, they teach us about a cell. While the banks are getting bailed, my homies are close to bail."* (Salaam-Bailey)

Here's another powerful quote from my good brother, Stix, which spoke to me, and I feel like it describes our current situation well. This idea of "sacred knowledge" is important for schools to know in order to fight against racism. Another thing that has been rendered illegal for some time now is racial discrimination in bank lending. Despite this, people of color still experience frequent denials when trying to loan money from banks, especially compared to their white counterparts. Even if they do get approved, they receive higher interest rates, which makes them feel discouraged to go through with the loan. Even in high income communities of color, the struggle for upward economic mobility is much more difficult than their white peers with the same level income, education and experience. When it comes to lending from banks, it seems like circumstances are always more complex and challenging to people of color. Ask yourself how might this impact a student's outlook on their future? I repeat, an access issue.

## Racial Profiling by Law Enforcement

This is something that we have been seeing a lot in recent months. Many say that racial profiling doesn't happen as blatantly as it did in the past, however, we have observed a new kind of racial profiling from law enforcement officers. Even simple things like wanting to use the restroom in some establishments can escalate rapidly until the person being discriminated against (usually someone of color) ends up in handcuffs. Sometimes, simply seeing a black man walking in a "nice neighborhood" can already cause alarm, only to find out that the individual actually lives in that neighborhood. These are some very common examples of ridiculous, but very realistic, instances of racial profiling. There has been a clear distinction between communities that are protected and served, and communities that are indeed enforced with law and order. As much as we want things to change, law enforcement can't seem to shake the massive array of "bad apples" that seems to have a very bad image of anyone who isn't white. I, as a black man with multiple degrees, am still a victim to 'DWB'–driving while black. A black man with a "nice car" pulled over because he "looks suspicious" is a sad reality. Students in our schools are also faced with the same reality.

These are just a few examples that clearly show why "Racism is like a deadly virus that mutates as systems change"—this is something I always say, and you can quote me on that. If we want things to change, then we have to do something about it. Even though things may appear to have gotten better for some of us, racism remains ingrained in society. And in education, institutional racism remains evident in terms of how differently white and black students are being treated. For instance, when black students and white students face similar challenges in school, the former is more likely to get either expelled or suspended. Because of this, we see that a disproportionate number of students being pulled from school are either African American, Native American, or Latino.

But we're not done yet! Although black students make up 16% of the total enrollment of students, 27% of these students are referred to law enforcement, while 31% of these students are subjected to arrest (Civil Rights Data Collection, 2014). On the other hand, white students make up 51% of the total enrollment, and 41% of these students are referred to law enforcement while 39% of them get arrested.

The racial differences in socioeconomic status, suspension rates, categorization into specialized courses or classes, advanced course-taking, and school funding all play roles in the challenges that students of color face in education. Sadly, this is the current state of our educational system, and if we don't take a stand, things cannot change for the better.

## The School to Prison Pipeline

*"To be a Negro in this country and to be relatively conscious is to be in a rage almost all the time." (Baldwin)*

Have you ever wondered why schools tend to involve law enforcement whenever black students need to be disciplined on school grounds?

Remember that 'Karens' and the ideology of racial discrimination exist in the classroom too, and they come in the form of teachers and principals across the nation. Even though black students and white students are of the same age and level, black students are often perceived to be more violent, and even older. Therefore, they are more likely to be disciplined at school. If this keeps happening, how do they continue to stay hungry for success? How can black students strive to be their best when they always have this fear of ending up excluded, suspended, or worse, in prison when they make a mistake?

This phenomenon, which is called the "school to prison pipeline", has become very rampant today. Let me remind you that systems are designed to get the results they get. How can black and brown students fully be accepted in a system that was designed for them to be excluded? This creatively evil design has caused black students and other students of color to practically expect unfair treatment from public schools and law enforcement, because this is what they see time and time again. Because of "zero tolerance" policies in schools, minor misbehaviors are being criminalized. When such things happen, cops are called in to discipline students, when these measures should only be handled within the school and by the school administration. Sadly, students of color are especially vulnerable to these discriminatory disciplinary applications and push-out trends, mainly due to the lack of building a true sense of belonging for students of color.

As a Revolutionary Educator, you shouldn't just sit back and accept this phenomenon, no matter how often it happens in your school. As part of your revolution, it's time for you to start BOOMIN'! It's time for you to take notice, stand up, and fight for all of your students.

The school to prison pipeline should not exist. PERIOD!

It should be a thing of the past. Something we have all taken part in dismantling. Something that we use as a lesson to bring awareness to how students of color were being suppressed and oppressed. If you can initiate this change in your school, you will be more than an educator— you will be a Revolutionary Educator! Someone who motivates, inspires, and fights for change. You will be someone who sees beyond the norms to discover the potential of all learners, no matter what color they might be, and you will be the agent of change, especially for students of color.

## Race in School

To discuss race in your school you must first begin with how race was developed. The concept of race was constructed and engineered by white men with a theory that falsely classified humans. Men like William Reade, who is famously known for his claim that Black Africans will be extinct in what he called Savage Africa. Then you have men like Robert Knox, who pretty much claimed that Black people were just inferior. In his book The Races of Men: A Fragment, Knox states that "there is a psychological inferiority in the dark races generally. This is perhaps not due to lack of size in the brain but rather a lack of quality in it." This theory was taken seriously and other men like Samuel Morton and many others contributed to the construction of race as a political structure and classification of humans that places non-whites as inferior and whites as superior. Our schools are still suffering from the impacts of these false claims.

## The Relationship Between Race, Poverty, and Education

If you have never lived in a world of poverty, you would never imagine how it can affect a student's ability to have critical hope. But, for a lot of students, this is the world they were born into, and it is the world they currently survive in. Many people in the city of Watts, California say Watts means, W-We A-Are T-Taught T-To S-Survive. Being a black student is already a huge challenge at school. But, being a black student who is also poor makes things seem impossible.

Poverty and critical hope have a very strong correlation with academic results. Most schools that have very low test scores typically have many students from families who live in poverty. This is not by accident. This is by design. Our current system is designed to have exceptions from the inner-city schools "make it", which leaves the community the same and everyone else behind. The reality is that students of color have a higher likelihood of attending high-poverty schools compared to Caucasian and even Asian-American students (National Center for Education Statistics, 2007).

Although the poverty rate for white people in America is at 10%, this rate is doubled for Latinx and Black people in America, and around 25% for native Indians in America. One of the main reasons for this difference is that people of color seem to have limited access in terms of employment opportunities, which is largely because of inequities that exist. Because of this, parents are faced with many complex challenges. Now, ask yourself: How might this impact your practice and your students' future role in society?

Hey, Revolutionary Educator, how can you say that you are educating the leaders of tomorrow when you cannot even bring racial injustices to light?

Personally, I believe that racism does not care about test scores. Racism could not care less about the amount of degrees you have. Instead, racism causes people to see only what is in front of them. And if they cannot get past this perspective, they will not see the potential and promise that lie beyond. Let us give equal and equitable opportunities to all students so that those who have been intentionally oppressed can have a fair chance to, you know, "pull themselves up by the bootstraps." We can start in our education system. Poverty, critical hope, and race shouldn't be hindrances in education. Even if you teach in a school where students come from poverty, educate those children as if you were a teacher of a highly regarded PWI Ivy League school! Better yet, educate your children as if your future depends on it. People might think you're crazy, but in the end, your students will reap everything you have sown as they learn how to believe in themselves, no matter what their backgrounds are. You will be the person that saves and transforms lives daily—Be Revolutionary!

## The Difference Between Educational Equity and Equality

*"One thing about the men that's controlling the pen that write history, they always seem to whiteout they sins." (J. Cole, 2018, Verse 2)*

The quote above is from the song, "Brackets", by one of my favorite artists, and when I heard those words, they spoke to me on such a profound level. These words speak about how the atrocities done in the past with regard to race have not been discussed or tackled in schools. These events seem to have been erased, or simply ignored, thus, the issues of the past have never been resolved until now, with you as that Revolutionary Educator. Think about it: if you had a conflict with someone and you never talked about it, would you be able to resolve the conflict?

No.

We all just suffer in silence knowing that the world right now seems alright, but if your eyes are open, or have been open, you would know the wounds inflicted on us, as a race, have never healed. To make themselves feel better, people talk about equality. But the truth is, especially in terms of education, what our students need is equity. For that reason and that reason only, I made the decision to no longer consider myself an "Instructional Leader" at my school. I was the Equity Leader. I didn't stop there. I also decided to change everything that began with the word instruction and changed it to equity. This meant we no longer had an instructional leadership team but it was now an equity leadership team. We no longer had instructional rounds, we had equity rounds. We no longer searched for instructional coaches, we searched for equity coaches. This language shift created a monumental shift in our actions towards leading with equity instead of equality. Although equality and equity are used interchangeably, they are two different things.

Equality refers to the way people are treated. In schools, this may translate as teachers providing all students with equal amounts of instruction or respect. Equality is generic, it focuses on the group as a whole, and it forces you to "see" everyone as equal. On the other hand, equity is all about supplying your students with the tools they individually require to thrive in school. Equity is adaptable and it allows you to focus on your students as individuals so that you show more fairness.

As a Revolutionary Educator, it is important for you to understand the distinction between these two terms. Since your students come from different backgrounds and have different advantages, it is up to you, as the teacher, to provide them with the tools and resources they need for their own unique circumstances. In some cases, you may have to put in more effort for some of your students to awaken their motivation and make them see that they are just as good, smart, and worthy as the other students in your class. While equality is valuable, equity in education is priceless!

## Revolution vs. Evolution

Before you can start your own revolution, you must understand what this powerful term means. It means for many of us we have to think differently, teach differently, and lead differently. Both evolution and revolution pertain to change. But while evolution is a gradual change that's bound to happen no matter what you do, revolution is the opposite. Revolution is a sudden drastic change that has the potential to effect positive change and acceleration. In the world of education, a revolution focuses on customization and adaptation. Instead of waiting for things to change, you will take the necessary steps to match the pace of your students and help them become the best versions of themselves.

By nature, revolution isn't a one-size-fits-all concept. It's not something that you can learn to do overnight. Initiating an education revolution takes a lot of brainstorming, planning, and reflecting. And you can do it in different ways. For instance, you can revolutionize the ways you help your students learn. Instead of trying to teach all of your students the same concepts at the same pace, you will focus on helping them learn what they need to at their own pace. This is having a student-centered approach around mastery learning. Although this may take more time, effort, and patience from you, this way of reaching out to your students allows you to focus on equity instead of equality.

Another way you can initiate a revolution is by changing the way you teach. These days, blended learning has become very popular. This approach combines traditional classroom teaching methods with the modern and innovative methods of online teaching. Although this approach may seem overwhelming and complex, learning how to become a teacher of blended learning will allow you to connect with your students in deeper and more relatable ways.

Right now, try to look at the current state of your school. Try to pinpoint the issues that are causing your students to fall behind or struggle. Once you have identified these issues, you can have your own brainstorming session where you would break free from traditions to initiate a drastic change—a revolution—to improve the different aspects of your school.

Yet another way to revolutionize your school is by focusing on the people who are teaching the students—the educators. What do you think could happen to the school system if talented teachers, principals, and other school leaders were paid more to stay at their schools instead of paying them more to leave the site and get a promotion? Most educators know that the real work is at the school-site. If we really solidify pay for educators, naturally, we will have a team of amazing individuals to work with at schools across the nation. Let's be real... compensation is very important. If your education was truly valued, then districts would pay their teachers properly. Then, you wouldn't have to search elsewhere for talented people because you'd already have them at your school. Revolutionize by pushing to pay your teachers, staff, and school leaders well, while giving them the resources they need to be the best they can be.

The world in which we live keeps changing, and we should always strive to keep up with the times. When you are faced with challenges, learn from them. When you see that your students are having a hard time, think of innovative ways to help them out. Your main goal for wanting to start a change is to make things better for yourself, your school, and your students who rely on you to light their path.

## It's Time for Revolutionary Education!

Many students are born as creators and explorers, but when they get to school, they are just told to sit down, shut up, and get in line. Today, many people feel that the education system has stopped teaching people how to critically think for themselves, and that it lacks real-life practical and creative skill-building. I challenge this idea by asking, "When did the system do anything different?" The education system has always focused on analytical intelligence and conformity ever since its origin. Therefore, many schools attempt to produce conformed minds who only know how to follow or do what they're told. According to experts, students these days only focus on passing their examinations instead of learning the material of their courses. And when you have teachers stick with archaic teaching methods and outdated pedagogy, this only exacerbates the issue. The reality for me is that the educational revolution should begin with reimagining all standardized tests. These tests are rooted in racism and fail to effectively include students of color. Standardized testing is a tool that ensures that inequities remain in our society. Standardized tests are the gatekeepers of access in many ways for students. The moment our system eliminates standardized testing will be the moment equity truly prevails.

The fact is, education remains to be a standardized way for students of different ages and levels to learn many concepts that they aren't interested in, and subjects that many won't be using in the future. Students who have amazing talents and great potential are forced into this standardized system to learn what they 'need', then work hard to pass their exams so that they can move forward. Just because this is the norm, should you simply accept this, or should you try to think of ways to revolutionize the educational system? To give you inspiration, here are some incredible examples for you:

- One organization decided to empower students by utilizing youth culture to elevate their learning. HipHopEd started their own revolution by curating an experience that intersects hip-hop, culture and education. I would be remiss if I didn't acknowledge the value hip-hop can have on a student's self-efficacy. Dr. Christopher Emdin leads this work with an amazing team that includes women like Dr. Courtney Rose who brings together a community of educators to challenge the status quo.

- A 19-year-old young woman by the name of Philippine Dolbeau has initiated her own educational revolution by coming up with ways to integrate simple digital solutions into the educational system. These help students by improving security in schools, while helping teachers improve their teaching and record-keeping methods. All these happen through an app called "NewSchool" that she created for a competition. Now, she is working with developers from Apple to refine the app to make it better.

- Meleah Lee Campbell more famously known as "Ms. Campbell," teaches on Instagram. She is a revolutionary educator who uses exceptional tools and software to analyze and enhance the way her students learn in class. She developed these tools with her colleagues to make learning accessible to anyone who wants to learn. This is an amazing way to reach out to students from different backgrounds.

- When I wrote this book, the world was in the throes of a global pandemic. During the pandemic, many educators had to try revolutionizing emergency distance-learning by providing students from all over the world with ways to further their education. Although virtual learning alone has also shown many inequities, there are educators who have creatively provided a great experience for their students in a virtual setting. This just shows that there is nothing that can impede the progress of a revolutionary educator.

As you can see, there are different ways to revolutionize the educational experience. Now is the right time to create a courageous educational framework that focuses on making an immediate and positive impact on your school to improve the learning outcomes of your students. As you do this, prepare yourself for some level of resistance. People and systems are often unwilling to accept change, especially when it comes suddenly and unexpectedly. But as long as you keep going, you keep inspiring, and you keep pushing for change, you will soon see the effects of your efforts paying off in ways that you never imagined possible!

## Take Time to Reflect

At the end of each chapter, you will get a chance to reflect on everything you have learned. Reflection is an important part of your learning process, as it allows you to gain a better understanding of what you have just read and how you can use this information to change your life. Although this is just the first chapter, you have already learned several concepts. Now, it's time to reflect.

Try to imagine yourself as a new principal of a school. You know that your plans and initiatives will only start having an effect in your third year. But in that same year, you will either get promoted, be released, or you will make the choice to move to another school. Knowing this, try to answer these questions:

- What would happen in your school if everything was focused on equity?

- What is the level of urgency you need to work with as soon as you start your role as a new principal?

- How can you make a more immediate change or impact in the school?

- How long do you need to determine if any of your strategies or initiatives are effective and efficacious?

- How are you making an impact on the lives of your staff and students each day?

Finding the answers to these questions will encourage you to think creatively and see the wider picture as you enter the next chapter...

# Chapter 2:

# Revolutionary Leadership for Student Achievement

*"You never change things by fighting the existing reality. To change something, build a new model that makes the existing model obsolete."* (Fuller)

To become a true revolutionary educator, you must be authentic, lead with equity and be unapologetic for the community in which you serve. As a black man who walks as his authentic self as a principal, I have been questioned about my integrity and character. Sadly, that comes with the territory. This happens quite often because I never fit the 'look' of a principal. As a revolutionary educator, you will be challenged so it becomes important that you prepare yourself mentally, spiritually, and physically. As a Black male educator, I always felt suppressed; I felt that I could never be my authentic self, and for many years, I have kept a chip on my shoulder because of it.

Schools and districts must be intentional about how they empower their Black male teachers. There is a reason that less than 5% of educators are Black men. For this reason, I promised myself that whenever I lead young people, I will let them see the possibilities. I will never forget the time when an older white teacher asked me how I became a principal. I thought to myself: What kind of question is that? Then I thought, just like everyone else! But deep down I felt that she wanted to know how did this black man become a founding principal at a young age and get to this level. As she glanced at my sneakers and fitted baseball hat, I could tell it was something she wasn't accustomed to seeing. She went on to ask me about what college I attended, at that moment I understood that I was as "foreign" to her as driving on the other side of the road.

I jokingly replied to her by saying I didn't finish college, I got my degree from the streets. I am a Neighborhood Scholar, a Street Intellectual that was selected to open this school because community-centered problems need to center members of the community for the solutions. Many educators that have reached the principalship still look for the solutions to their school's practical problems from some program established by a professor from an Ivy League or some well-established, predominantly white institution.

Well, that PhD, EdD, or any other letters that reinforce a certain 'standard' of intelligence, do not equip anyone with the ability to solve the everyday problems of our community and schools. I knew she was wondering how I overcame all the barriers that were supposed to strip my "urban" views. I was supposed to assimilate and conform. She probably thought, how did the system lose? The standardized test scores, the interviews, colleges, and universities with the exams were supposed to ensure that I, as a leader of society, will walk, talk, act, and write, to a certain 'standard'. Let this be a reminder that no matter how hard you work or how many degrees you have, the story of 'they' will still exist. They want you to be a certain way, speak a certain way, walk, and dress a certain way. So, know that when you are being revolutionary for the community and walking as your authentic self, it will be feared. Be prepared for this. I remember after explaining this to a mentee, she asked, "When did this mindset shift happen for you?" I responded, "Well, it happened when I surrendered the outcome and focused on my purpose and mission."

You should learn how to become a leader. Revolutionary leadership is essential to move your school forward, inspire change, and motivate your students to seek excellence in their studies. In this chapter, you will learn how to become an effective leader who inspires everyone around you to stay hungry until you achieve your goal of helping your students become the best versions of themselves. It's not your job to sit back and relax. It's your calling to take a stand and make things better

## Becoming a Revolutionary Leader

Revolutionary leadership is essential for you to improve the academic achievement in your school and achieve change that will last for the foreseeable future. Becoming a revolutionary leader enables you to help your school improve. But for this, you must first understand what being a revolutionary leader really means.

Knowing when and how to follow is a fundamental leadership competency. As a revolutionary leader, your ability to follow is critical. As a revolutionary leader, you must also learn how to become more empathetic toward the people around you. This gives you a better understanding of who they are and what they can bring to the table. This level of understanding will increase your effectiveness, promote flexibility, and make you more adept at engaging others. To become a revolutionary leader, you must learn how to:

- Develop genuine relationships and nurture them.

- Create a culture of positivity, collaboration, and open communication.

- Communicate with everyone—and I mean everyone!

- Inspire the people around you—even other leaders.

- Nurture the unique personalities, talents, and skills of others.

- Keep track of your school's environment at all times. Never stop building your community.

- Maintain visibility and an air of openness.

- Allow your staff to lead to make things better. Don't be afraid of failure.

- Acknowledge and accept when you make mistakes.

- Celebrate achievements no matter how small.

As a revolutionary leader, you should also be a good role model. Commit to the task of being this kind of leader so that the people around you know that you are in it for the long haul. I will say this again: Revolutionary leaders also know how to be adaptive and have the ability to adjust to different kinds of situations. For instance, if you are working on a project wherein one member of your team has more experience and expertise than you do, you can adjust your role and become a follower. This is what you call putting progress ahead of pride.

To be able to do all these things, you must first have self-awareness. You should learn how to recognize how you feel about interacting, thinking, and reasoning with others. This self-awareness will help guide you as you work towards becoming an effective leader that everyone will want to follow.

## Keys to Revolutionary Leadership

By understanding what a revolutionary leader is, you can start taking the necessary steps to become one. Your journey towards becoming this kind of leader will take time and a lot of effort from you. But if you can achieve this, you will not only improve yourself, but everyone else around you, too.

As a revolutionary leader, you need to learn to connect with those around you. Personally, I have a philosophy called the "3Rs." That stands for Relationships, Relevance, and Rigor, each of which can be applied to your leadership journey as follows:

- Whenever you build **relationships**, you must have an intent of belonging. This gives you an important purpose, while encouraging you to show your true self to others

- Having an intent and purpose brings **relevance** to your efforts. As you connect with others, you will see the importance of these relationships, especially as you try to become a leader.

- Finally, you must strive to put **rigor** into your leadership, the attention to detail with a certain standard of excellence. As others see this enthusiasm, they will understand that you are working with them to improve your staff, your students, and your entire school.

The great thing about the 3Rs is that you can apply them to all aspects of your school. As you keep these in your mind, let us go through some strategies you can use to become a revolutionary leader:

- **Create an ideal learning environment**

    This is very helpful for both educators and students. Before you can improve the learning environment of your students, you must first make things better for your teachers. Find ways to eliminate teacher resistance, negativism, and defeatism— things that make it extremely challenging for teachers to educate with passion and enthusiasm.

    If you can build better relationships with your teachers and create a warm school community, you will start seeing an amazing change happening in your school. When this happens, your teachers will be more willing to improve the learning environments and experiences they give to the students. It's a win-win situation!

- **Create a vision of academic success for all of your students**

After creating a more conducive learning environment, the next thing for you to target is the academic success of your students. For this, you have to work with your teachers to find ways to improve instruction, as well as your school's goals for student progress.

You must work rigorously and relentlessly to improve the quality of instruction by setting higher standards, and helping your teachers identify and accept student achievement in forms of creative and practical intelligence as well. In addition, you will have to inspire and encourage your teachers to continue their professional learning efforts to make them more effective educators. Work closely with your staff and teachers to generate new, innovative strategies for instructional approaches that will engage your students and make them more intrinsically motivated to learn.

- **Teach others how to lead and cultivate their abilities**

Another way to become a revolutionary leader is by teaching others how to become revolutionary too. While good leaders know how to manage their staff, great leaders know how to cultivate their staff. For instance, department heads or aspiring leaders on campus should feel inspired to lead the teachers in their department. The leadership team should be collectively ready to have training, seminars, practical exercises, and other professional development activities with you because they know they will be filled with great learning opportunities. And when the people around you see that you want them to learn how to become leaders, and that you trust them enough to want them to succeed, this will make them feel valued.

- **Effectively manage information, processes, and people to promote improvement in your school**

  Being a revolutionary leader doesn't just apply to how you deal with the people around you. It's also important for you to learn how to manage all other aspects of your school, such as processes, information, and other resources. You have to focus on all aspects of your school if you want to make things better. For this, you need to come up with your own management strategies to make sure that you aren't leaving anything out

  Becoming a revolutionary leader is a journey. Take your time with it and learn everything you can from it. Soon, you won't even realize that you have transitioned into this role, and that it has become a valuable facet of your life as an educator.

## Mission-Driven vs. Career-Driven

Right now, take a moment to think about what drives you.

Are you driven by your mission, or are you driven by your career? A career-driven person focuses mainly on working towards their own personal goals, such as achieving a certain pay grade, or a specific rank or position. Once you reach this goal, you might not feel as passionate about your job anymore.

On the other hand, being a mission-driven person allows you to go beyond the surface so that you can discover the 'how' and 'why' of your organization's existence. A friend of mine, Dennis McKesey, a former principal, had a 'why' to improve school leadership off of school grounds, so he decided to start a leadership movement for principals called, "Off School Grounds," or 'OSG'. His mission has supported leaders to further their mission on and off their school grounds. Naturally, if you want to make a difference as a revolutionary leader, you must aim to become a mission-driven leader. Then, you can work towards the mission of your school to achieve a higher purpose.

If you love what you do and you have a passion for it, you can easily become a mission-driven leader. As a mission-driven leader, you can help the people around you become mission-driven individuals too. If you can encourage everyone else in your school to be mission-driven, you will see higher levels of engagement and productivity. Mission-driven educators also have a greater likelihood of staying with their school as they evolve into amazing high performers. By understanding the mission and purpose of your school, the people who work with you will have more investment in your school. Instead of feeling like they are simply working in your school, they will feel like they belong there. This makes it easier for them to work happily, enthusiastically, and with high motivation. Now that you know all these wonderful things that can come from being driven by your mission, ask yourself, "Am I a mission-driven leader?"

If you feel like you already have a passion for your work and your role as a leader, you may already be on your way to becoming a mission-driven leader. Still, there are things you can do to improve yourself and ultimately, transform those around you. Here are a few ways you can do this:

- **Conduct a survey to discover who are career-driven and who are mission-driven in your school**

  Creating a survey for your staff (both returning and new) allows you to learn more about them. Although this may take some effort on your part, you will gain a wealth of information from the responses you get from these surveys. Try not to make it into a big deal. Just tell your staff or team that you want to learn more about them and how you can support their goals as a professional. As you read the completed survey forms, take note of the common responses. You can use the information you get to determine who is already mission-driven and who needs to be encouraged more to go past their personal goals to become more valuable members of your team. Remember, every team member has value.

- **Ask questions as you communicate with others**

  One of the best ways to discover more about the people you work with is by asking them relevant questions about their work, how they see the school, how happy they are with what they are doing, and whether or not they have seen your school's mission in action. Throw these questions into your conversations once in a while to get the answers you need without making others feel intimidated.

- **Have brainstorming sessions about how you can emphasize the mission of your school**

  Finally, you can conduct regular brainstorming sessions to discuss the mission of your school and how to make it part of your daily lives (both for you as educators and your students). You can do this during your meetings, or you can set a specific schedule that is only meant for this purpose. These regular brainstorming sessions help everyone become familiar with your mission, while encouraging them to think of ways to emphasize your school's mission. Eventually, this can help change how your employees think, to become more mission-driven too.

## Take Time to Reflect

The reality is this: the "traditional" principal has gotten us to this point. The state of education in which we currently are, is a product of what happens 'traditionally'. Traditional thinking has failed our children. We need more people disrupting tradition–not praising it. We need you to be Revolutionary.

Throughout my journey as an educator, I have met many people from all walks of life. Whenever I meet new people, I make it a point to ask about their own journeys. I am always interested to hear how people— especially educators and leaders—have grown and evolved into who they have become when I meet them. To wrap up this chapter and help you reflect on what you have learned, let me share a story with you.

During one of the many conferences I have attended, I met this school leader who turned their whole school around by implementing a series of small, seemingly insignificant strategies. The great thing about these strategies this school leader implemented is that they made an immediate impact on their school. In turn, this helped move the turnaround process along. When I asked what these strategies were, this amazing school leader gave the following examples:

- Creating open and welcoming communication channels between educators and parents.

- Asking the teachers to give suggestions to improve the school, and then implementing those suggestions.

- Providing simple in-house training and seminars to improve the perceived weaknesses of the teachers and staff.

Simple, right?

These are just some examples of how a school was changed in a short span of time. As a leader in your school (whether you already hold a leadership role or you want to become an effective leader sometime in the future), ask yourself the following reflective questions, while keeping in mind everything you learned in this chapter:

- Who am I?

- Why am I here?

- What do I represent?

- How will I lead?

By answering these questions through self-reflection, you can kick-start your leadership journey. But we are not done yet; there is still much for you to learn on your path toward revolutionizing education...

# Chapter 3:

# The Challenges of Changing the Current Educational System

*"I'm not saying I'm gonna change the world, but I guarantee that I will spark the brain that will change the world." (Shakur)*

Becoming a Revolutionary Leader who makes amazing changes in your school won't be an easy task. You will have to deal with—and overcome—a number of challenges. These challenges are the roadblocks that face you and all other educators in America. When you try to make changes in your own school, you may discover that it won't be as easy as you thought, because you are held back by policies and systemic hurdles. Even though you would like to improve your school, you must first understand that you will be faced with overcoming obstacles embedded within the current school system.

## The 5 Obstacles in Revolutionizing Education

For you to overcome the obstacles and challenges of the current school system, you must first know what they are. Then, you can come up with a plan for how to overcome them. In this chapter, we will go through the most common challenges, including the ones that are most difficult to deal with. If you can overcome these, dealing with other obstacles will be a lot easier. So let's get you BOOMIN'!

## The Issue of Opposition

Opposition may come in many forms and from different sources. As you try to lead and make positive changes, you might experience resistance and opposition from your district or school leaders, your colleagues, your students' parents, and other members of your community. This reaction is known to most educators who try to initiate new practices and approaches. I, myself, have experienced opposition, and it almost made me give up.

Almost.

Of course, I wouldn't be where I am right now if I just gave in to everyone who opposed me. Instead, I came up with a plan for how to ease the negativity and turn the people who opposed me into people who supported me. Here are some of the most effective ways I achieved this:

- Start by finding mentors. Establish and develop deep relationships with them, especially with the people who are part of or associated with your school. Always take the opportunity to reach out to others, especially to people you believe might offer constructive feedback.

- Start with easy, small-scale approaches that will inform everyone about the more comprehensive initiatives you're planning for the future.

- Provide your teachers and staff with internal opportunities for professional development. Through these opportunities, you can demonstrate the effectiveness of the new practices and approaches you want to make.

- As you present the new approaches, practices, and strategies, also provide external evidence of how effective they are. You can also do this while you are implementing the changes.

- Consider giving shared leadership a try. Identify the people in your school who will potentially show resistance, and then show them how the new strategies work. You can also practice modeling these strategies and asking these people to get involved in the implementation of the strategies.

You should create a vision for staff investment to make it easier for everyone to accept and support your ideas.

## Putting All Responsibility on You as the Leader

This particular issue is very frustrating to experience and difficult to overcome. It happens when you realize that everyone in your school relies on you, their leader, for direction and suggestions for change. Although this might seem like a good thing for you because it means that the people you lead look up to you, they might still oppose your ideas or suggestions, even if they've asked for such in the first place.

Being a Revolutionary Leader comes with a sense of pride, but not when everyone else around you isn't putting in any kind of effort, or are deeply rooted in problem-based practices, opposed to solution-based practices. I personally believe in and practice the 7 principles of the Nguzo Saba. One of those principles is called 'Ujima', which means collective work and responsibility. Being a leader can be a tiring experience. To overcome this, you must learn how to transform your leadership into something shared, collective, and extended. Learn how to delegate your tasks to build capacity for improvement and change. Introduce these concepts to the people around you instead of trying to do everything yourself just so they won't oppose you. Remember, if everyone does a little, no one person has to do a lot.

This kind of leadership is called distributive leadership, and it's an important part of improved organizational outcomes. As you practice this kind of leadership, it will help contribute to the growth and learning of the people you lead. When things improve for everyone, this can even have a positive effect on the performance and achievement of your students.

## Putting Up with Mandated Policies

As much as you would like to inspire changes in your school, you still have to put up with mandated policies. These refer to policies that specifically dictate what you're supposed to teach, and when you're supposed to teach these things. In some cases, these policies might even be more strict and specific depending on the type of school you're in. For instance, if you work in a school where you give your teachers scripts of what they should say in class, then you truly need to make a lot of changes. Teacher autonomy matters.

Sadly, the current structures of schools, from the curriculum to the physical facilities, create and sustain a fragmented educational experience. This doesn't just apply to students, but to teachers too. To change this, you must aim to create a holistic curricular experience founded in sacred knowledge for your teachers and students. For many decades, such a concept has been through cycles of acceptance and rejection. But if you can convince those around you to embrace this sacred approach, then you won't have to put up with mandated policies. Instead, you can have your own! I call this doing what you have to do, so you can do what you want to do!

## Insufficient Resources

Here's another challenge that can be difficult to overcome. Without enough funding or resources, it can be very difficult to get your hands on new materials and curriculum materials for your teachers to use. This is even more difficult when you have large class sizes, with students who are at different academic levels. Fortunately, there are things you can do to help your teachers deal with insufficient resources. Here are some examples:

- If you don't have enough materials for all of the students in the class, you and your teachers can start producing creative stories to share on social media in order to raise funds for materials. People invest in stories. This is also a principle of the Nguzo Saba, called 'Ujamaa'—cooperative economics. By doing this, your students won't have to rely solely on their textbooks, which lack sacred knowledge anyway. Instead, they will have everything they need to achieve absolute excellence.

- If your teachers don't have access to multimedia devices to enhance the learning of your students, come up with a strategic campaign to write to companies that you think would be willing to donate to support. Have you ever heard the phrase, "a closed mouth doesn't get fed"? Well, buckle down and write to companies such as Microsoft, Apple, Google, and other tech giants to see if they will be willing to support your mission. The worst they can do is say no. If some of your teachers, parents, and students participate in the campaign too, this will have a greater impact on community participation. In turn, this increases the likelihood of the donation manifesting. Make sure you highlight the campaign by having everyone share your story. By doing this, you will create a movement while also building community.

Although insufficient resources are a real problem, there are things you can do to make things better. As you can probably tell, one of the main things that I do is creatively fundraise through social media and other events, such as having a gala or selling school limited-edition items, or just simply asking organizations to donate to our school. If you can enlist the help of those around you without opposition, this problem becomes much easier to solve.

## Lack of Communication

Without effective communication, starting a revolution would be almost impossible. To make positive changes, you need to communicate openly with your district or school leaders, your colleagues, your students' parents, and other members of your community. I personally have adopted work from Patrick Lencioni. In his book, The Advantage: Why Organizational Health Trumps Everything Else In Business, he identifies the importance of communication as creating clarity, reinforcing clarity, and over-communicating clarity. In other words, communicate, communicate, communicate. If you want communication to lead to support instead of opposition, here are some tips for you:

- Communicate openly with everyone and do this as early and as often as possible. Encourage two-way communication wherein you take turns sharing ideas and listening to each other.

- As much as possible, communicate face-to-face. Although text messages and emails are quick and efficient, there is nothing more effective than talking to people in person. If you do opt to communicate through text messages or emails, make sure to give a reply within a reasonable timeframe. This shows that you value communication and that you aren't too busy to make time for others.

- When communicating, get straight to the point. Try not to waste other people's time by giving long-winded speeches when your message is very brief.

- Communication shouldn't end with you. Even though you are the leader of your school, you shouldn't be the only one who communicates well. Elevate your staff to communicate well too. That way, people will always have a good experience no matter who they speak to in your school.

- Offer parents opportunities to provide feedback for your school. This makes them feel more open and trusting. When the parents see that you want to make things better, and that you are willing to involve them in the process, their trust in you and the school grows.

- As parents feel more trusting and positive toward you and the rest of the school, you can help them understand how important they are in the students' education. Help them see how you must work hand-in-hand toward student achievement by supporting each other.

You can also use different forms of communication, verbal and written, to reach out to a wider audience. For instance, you can send messages and important information through social media platforms, newsletters, blogs, or even mobile apps. If you can establish open, respectful communication with others, achieving your goals can become simpler and more enjoyable.

## Take Time to Reflect

As a leader and an educator, challenges and obstacles will always be part of your journey. But what will set you apart from the rest is how you face these challenges and overcome them. Every time I feel like I am drowning in challenges and I need inspiration to save me, I read about inspiring leaders and educators who have overcome such amazing challenges to make sure that their students don't fall behind.

One school in Newark, New Jersey had challenges around food and bullying. The Principal there, Akbar Cook, started two programs to revolutionize the experiences for his students. He placed washers and dryers in the school to assist students with clothes and also started a "Lights On Program" that supports students having a place to go in the evening hours to be safe while having food and shelter. Because of this, hundreds of students' lives have been saved and transformed. This not only helped the students learn better, but it also allowed them to decrease the amount of students who were losing their lives due to gun violence on the streets.

As you can see, there will always be a way for you to make things better. Now, as you reflect at the end of this chapter, try to answer these questions:

- What obstacles are in the way of my goal to transform the system?

- Who are the stakeholders whose buy-in I need to push the transformational agenda?

- How can I support my teachers and school staff to achieve the goals of our school?

- How do I tackle the challenges of revolutionizing the educational experience?

# Chapter 4:

# Organizational Culture as a Foundation for Student Achievement

*"The walls of a school should reflect a future possibility. The halls should honor dreams. The rooms to help prepare for them."* (Wolpert-Gawron)

Have you ever thought about what kind of culture you have created in your school?

Culture is a very important aspect of school life since it serves as the foundation for your student's achievement. With the right kind of culture, you can have inspiring and motivating educators in your school. Naturally, this will ingrain a sense of pride and belonging to bring your students together and motivate them to do their best in all aspects of their learning. Here, you will learn the importance of culture and how to build the right kind of culture for the benefit of your school.

## What is Organizational Culture?

The organizational culture of your school is very important. By definition, organizational culture refers to a set of common norms, attitudes, and values. Within this set, some of the norms, attitudes, and values are explicit, while others are not. The culture of your organization also defines the "right way" to do things. If you need this to hit you more, I want you to ask yourself what is "the (insert your school's name) way" of doing things? By knowing this culture and introducing it to the people you lead, you can shape their behaviors, understanding, and perceptions.

Organizational culture has an impact on all aspects of your school. When everyone in your school aligns with its culture, they will feel more appreciated, supported, and more comfortable too. This is because a school's organizational culture:

- Provides you with a strong sense of identity. This is essential for your employees to feel like they are making a difference by doing their best as educators.

- Helps shape the patterns of behavior and the expected standards in your school. Without these, you might experience a lot of chaotic occurrences in your school.

- Creates specific ways of accomplishing things to make it clearer for everyone.

- Encourages "achievement orientation" wherein teachers and students develop the passion and drive to do their best, accomplish their goals, and find success in life.

- Determines your school's direction for future progression and growth.

One thing you must remember about organizational culture is that it isn't stagnant. Over time, you and your team can develop a new set of norms, attitudes, and values regarding what you think is right for your school at that moment. When you discover that some things don't work, you may have to change them. This is essential if you want your school's culture to remain relevant. However, changing your school's culture isn't a simple task. You might encounter resistance once again. As a leader, you must show everyone why there is a need for this change, what benefits you will gain from it, and how to make the change happen.

## Positive vs. Negative Organizational Culture

The culture you build in your school can either be positive or negative.

Since culture has a profound effect on your teachers, staff, and students, you want to focus on creating a positive school culture. Before you can do that, let's take a look at these two types of cultures and how different they are from another.

## *Positive School Culture*

A positive school culture promotes effectiveness, high performance, and professional satisfaction. With such a culture, everyone in your school will always strive and stay hungry. Creating a positive school culture means creating a learning environment that focuses on collaboration and collegiality. You celebrate successes whether they come from your teachers or students. You also commit yourself to empower your teachers and students by making sure that their learning never stops.

As I was thinking of ways to create a positive school culture, I thought, "What if we collectively treated every student like we knew they were going to be the next big thing?" When I asked this question to my teachers, it got them thinking. And together, we worked to create a conducive environment and a positive culture.

Such a culture will make everyone in your school believe that they have what it takes to reach their goals. With this kind of thinking, everything will work like clockwork and you will notice your school growing, evolving, and transforming into something more than what it was when you started.

## Negative School Culture

Negative school culture is the complete opposite, as it is characterized by resistance to collaboration and evident inefficiency. In such a school, colleagues don't trust each other, the leader doesn't exhibit transparency, and educators have very little academic support for their students. And when students don't excel, or worse, when they fail at their subjects, teachers blame them for not trying hard enough.

Negative school culture is toxic. Within the school, teachers and staff tend to get into a lot of conflicts with one another until they end up becoming hostile towards each other. This type of culture is heavy, negative, and it won't lead to any kind of growth. In such a culture, reform will become exponentially more difficult.

Therefore, if you want your school to succeed, you must establish and nurture a positive school culture. Such a culture requires effective leadership, attention to your goals, and genuine teamwork with all stakeholders. This will help shape your school's culture, as well as its organizational structure.

## How to Shape Your School's Organizational Culture

Now that you understand the concept of school culture, you know how important it is in the growth and progress of your school. To understand your own school's culture, you must know its leverage points and roadblocks. Leverage points refer to the things within your school where creating a small change in them can initiate a huge impact. For instance, one leverage point in your school can be the ability to provide your teachers with some autonomy to find or create learning materials. Through professional development, you can show your teachers how to do these things with great intentionality and deliberateness. If they learn successfully, they can improve the learning experience of their students and impact student outcomes.

On the other hand, roadblocks are the things that might prevent you from making progress. For instance, a lack of resources is a significant roadblock. But with a little creativity and collaboration, you can overcome this along with your team. Another way to understand your school's culture is by recognizing and acknowledging your school's current status—where it is right now. In the process of doing this, you should also recognize and acknowledge the past (Sankofa)–everything that has brought you to this current moment. After understanding the culture of your school, it's time to take steps to shape a new, revolutionary school culture. Here are some ways for you to do this:

- Start by creating the capacity to change. You need a team for this. You can either work with your whole staff, or a select group of people first. Together, make a list of what works well in your school and appreciate all these things. Then make a list of what doesn't work, along with what changes you want to see.

- As you work with others, invest in them. Take them on a retreat out of the school environment. Wine and dine them with love. While doing this, you then provide them with opportunities to share their expertise. Encourage teachers to collaborate by creating a professional learning community in your school. These meetings and gatherings work well at hotels with a great ambiance and food. Trust me, it works.

- Create and send surveys to teachers, students, and parents about their experiences with the school. You can also host community forums for the same purpose. This gives you a lot of insight into the culture of your school and how to improve it.

- Think of educational experiences and events that focus on celebrating and honoring ethnic, linguistic, and racial differences. Appreciating cultural diversity is an amazing way to promote positivity.

- Provide your teachers with learning experiences that focus on identity, emotional regulation, self-efficacy, and self-management—these are essential issues that arise in our schools today. Then, your teachers can share what they have learned with the students to reduce the instances of bullying, while increasing the ability for your students to achieve self-actualization at school and create a more positive culture.

- Create a looping advisory program where you pair students with adult advisors. Offer this to all students, not just those who feel like they are struggling in any aspect of their lives. All students should be assigned to an advisor so that they can create deeper ties with one another. Personally, I recommend a minimum 2-year loop. At my school, our students are paired with their kinship (advisory) teacher for all four years.

- Develop a leadership team that consists of teachers, school administrators, parents, student leaders, and even other members of the community.

As you work to shape your school's organizational culture and structure, you might come up with your own bright ideas for how to make things better. Of course, each school has its own strengths and areas of growth. As you discover those, you can create your own unique plan with your team.

# Take Time to Reflect

Culture is an important part of our lives. In a school setting, culture is a significant aspect that defines how you, your teachers, staff, and students function within the walls of the school. As a leader, you have to help everyone understand the value of culture. If needed, you must develop a school culture that supports the educational processes and the values that you want everyone to value. To do this, you should ask yourself the following questions for self-reflection:

- What are the central values of your school as an organization?

- Does your school encourage professional development activities that support the understanding and development of your school's organizational culture?

- How does your school ensure that different understandings of basic values are confronted and discussed?

- How does your school ensure that students understand the school's basic values?

- How does your school engage your students in the development of the school's culture? In other words, what is your students' role in it?

# Chapter 5:

# Principle 1: Setting the Stage

*"If you don't know where you are going, how can you expect to get there?"* (Sankofa)

After reading the first four chapters and taking time to reflect after each chapter, you are now ready to start your journey of revolution. For this, you need to understand the six basic principles that will help you unlock the hidden potential of your school. In this chapter, we will discuss the first principle—setting the stage. Here, you will learn how to create the vision, mission, philosophy, and goals for your school to work towards.

## Building Your Game Plan

Building a game plan for success is a complex process. This game plan should focus on creating a moment to build a movement. You don't just take half an hour out of your day to create a game plan that will work. Take, for instance, the best sports teams that have won championships. The members of that team don't just play using their own individual strategies. Instead, they think of and agree with effective strategies as a team. In other words, they work together for one common goal.

Therefore, as you try to create a game plan for your school, you need to include the people around you. For this, you need to establish a culture of action, innovation, and excellence. You need to be an inspiration to others so that you can bring them together to strive for a single mission. YOU MUST BE THE INSPIRATIONAL

LEADER! To prepare yourself, consider implementing the following tips:

- **Attitude Matters!**

  Whenever you want to do something, you should always have the right attitude. Even if you have an amazing plan, if you don't have the attitude to go with it, there is very little chance of success. On the other hand, if you just have a rough plan for what you want to accomplish but you approach your journey with enthusiasm and positivity, you will keep going no matter what happens.

- **School positional scan**

  Before creating your game plan, evaluate yourself and your school. Take a look at what you already have. This helps you determine what you need. Also, knowing your strengths gives you a better idea of how to approach certain tasks, challenges, and strategies.

- **Stay hungry**

  On the flip side, you should also know what you lack. To stay hungry as a leader is to be honest with yourself and be humble enough to know that you are not perfect. That's the smart thing to do. After all, you wouldn't be on this journey in the first place if you believed that there isn't anything wrong with the education system, right? Once you acknowledge and accept your weaknesses, you can start your own BOOM effect as you motivate yourself to keep learning.

- **Accept failure**

  Yes, failure will always be part of your journey. I would say one of my best qualities as a Principal is that I am not afraid of failure, but like the rapper, Chance the Rapper, always says,

"Turn your L's [losses] into lessons." Even with an amazingly well-thought-out plan, you may experience a bump or two in the road. Learning how to accept failure makes everything easier. Accept it, learn from it, and move on.

- **Lead with grace**

  Right now, as you read this book, you already have the potential to make great changes. With your passion and drive, you already have the potential to start a revolution that will change things for the better. Appreciate yourself. Learn to be grateful for where you are right now. If you're in a position to lead others, use that to your advantage. If not, take this time to learn everything you can so that you will be fully prepared when you achieve a leadership role in the future.

- **Just do it!**

  You may have already heard this slogan (it's from Nike) and simple as it is, these three words are extremely powerful. Instead of just planning to create your game plan, take the time to do it! Only then can you move forward with your plans and take the steps to achieve your goals.

## Creating a Revolutionary Mantra

The term "mantra" is Sanskrit, and it means "sacred thought" or "sacred utterance." In a religious or spiritual context, a mantra is a phrase that you repeat to yourself to facilitate your transformation. But in a more contemporary context—like in business or in a school—your mantra is like your motto or marketing slogan. It is something simple, powerful, and memorable. And it is important for your revolutionary transformation.

The key to creating an amazing mantra for your school is simplicity. Think of a mantra with just two to three words to make it more fun and memorable. For instance, phrases like, "Don't be evil" or "Think different" will already get your mind working, especially when you try to connect these mantras to the companies that created them— Google and Apple, Inc.

Your school's mantra isn't the same as its mission statement. The main purpose of creating a revolutionary mantra is to start a movement.

You want to make changes, so you need to have something that people will keep repeating to highlight the changes you are trying to initiate. Combining an amazing mantra with a specific purpose and intention will clarify, amplify, and enhance the results of your efforts.

For centuries, different organizations, teams, and even tribes have created mantras to inspire, elevate, and motivate. From military groups to businesses to non-profit organizations, sports teams, and more, all the mantras they have created have made an impact on the internal culture of our world. By creating your own revolutionary mantra for your school, it will serve as a guide for the strategies you make for the future. It will also tell the world more about your school and its culture.

As you try to come up with your mantra, remember to keep it short and sweet. A line that's too long won't be effective, as people won't even bother to remember it. Right now, you might not think that a simple phrase will make an impact. But, once you create the phrase that will define your school and put it out there, you will see how much it affects you, your teachers, your students, and your school's image. My school has adopted the mantra, "LET'S BOOM", and it has completely shifted the language and culture at our school. Students and staff use this mantra to motivate and acknowledge greatness on our campus. If you ever visit our school, it is not uncommon to hear students say "Let's BOOM" or "we are

BOOMIN'" on campus. This language is part of the DNA of our school.

If you haven't considered creating a mantra for your school, now is the time to do so. While you can do this yourself, you also have the option to invite other members of your team to help you out. Choose the most passionate people, the ones whom you know will help you create a mantra that will make a huge impact on anyone who hears, sees, or shares it. Also, make sure it's completely original so that people won't confuse your school with some other organization or company!

## Developing Your School's Mission and Vision

Developing the mission and vision of your school is an essential step towards creating a successful movement. By creating a great mission and a realistic vision, you will give your school direction and clarity. On the other hand, a vague mission and a muddy vision might create conflict in your school, as the people around you won't know how to identify what matters most.

But, before you can create these two important things, you must first understand what they are. The mission of your school provides an overview of the steps you need to take to achieve your goals for the future. The mission is longer and more explanatory compared to the vision. The vision of your school is how you hope to see it in the future. In other words, it is your school's goal. When thinking about this, make sure it's short, sweet, and easy to remember.

Creating the vision of your school doesn't have to be your sole responsibility. You can call in valuable members of your team to help you out. Before you say, "Let's BOOM!" you may want to share some examples to them to help them understand what a vision is. To start off, here are some excellent examples you can share:

- At John T. Baker Middle School (Maryland), their vision is, "To establish a thinking, caring community of learners for life."

- At Battlefield High School (Virginia), their vision is, "Every Battlefield High School student will achieve personal success and become a responsible and productive citizen."

- At my school, it is, "All students will be positive agents of change by achieving self-actualization."

After sharing these vision statements with your team (and others you have researched on your own), give them some time to reflect. Then initiate a discussion for how to create or remake your school's vision statement. For this, you can ask the following questions:

- Why do you need a new vision for your school? (Ask this if you have an existing vision statement and you'd like to change it)

- What do you like or dislike in your school's current vision? (Ask this if you have an existing vision statement and you'd like to change it)

- How can you make a vision that's specific, easy to understand, and easy to remember?

- How can you make a vision that expresses hope for your school's future?

- What are the expectations that come with your school's new vision?

- How can you encourage everyone in your school so support the new vision you will make for your school?

After creating your school's new vision, try to determine whether or not you can make this vision happen. Of course, if your school already has a powerful vision statement, then you may choose to simply tweak it a bit to make it stand out. The point here is to have a school vision (and mission) that everyone working in your school will see as their common direction, as a statement that inspires them to be the best they can be. It should also express to your students and parents where your school is headed and why they should be there to take the journey with you.

When you have created the best possible vision for your school, then you can move on to creating your school's mission. This is where you would start elaborating your vision statement and breaking it down into steps. Your mission would be to achieve that vision by working together as a school.

## Thinking of Your School's Academic Philosophy and Core Values

Right now, what is your school's academic philosophy?

Another important aspect of setting the stage for your revolution so you can BOOM is to find out what truly matters for you, to determine your school's academic philosophy. Some of the most common school philosophies include values such as kindness, honesty, respect, cooperation, hard work, and compassion. Of course, different schools have different values. As a leader, you have to help your school determine which values are most important to you so you can set a framework on determining your philosophy.

Having core values will help you communicate the mission, standards, desired outcomes, and the story of your school. Establishing these values will lead to better expectations and standards as to what type of culture and atmosphere you want to nurture in your school. Be creative with these values. For example, at my school, we call our core values "THE BOOM 5". These values are U-Respect, U-Love, U-Work Hard, U-Follow-Through, U-Get Results. If you do all five of those, then U-BOOM! The U-BOOM is the bonus value, as more of a symbol of absolute excellence. The core values of your school will also provide you with a way of thinking, in terms of the educational initiatives and philosophies you will support.

At the end of the day, establishing core values and a collective academic philosophy will help make your school community stronger. But the challenge here is that determining and establishing both isn't as easy as you might think. The good news is you can simplify the process by following these essential steps:

- **Have a brainstorming session**

  The first thing you must do is make a list of values that you think describe your school. After that, you can have a brainstorming session with your staff to help you narrow down the list. Ask them which values are most important to them. Then, you can come up with your final list of values by involving your students and their families in the process. Determining the philosophy of your school isn't something you should do yourself. Your school is made up of teachers, staff, students, parents, and families. To establish the best and most relevant academic philosophy, you will need their input too. This will take a lot of time, effort, and patience on your part, but it will all be worth it in the end.

- **Establish a "community code" for your school**

  Now that you have your academic philosophy and a set of values, you should think of ways to connect them to your school community. To do this, you have to come up with phrases or sentences that explain why you have chosen this philosophy and set of values, and how they apply to your school. Make sure that the messages you create are consistent, clear, and thought-provoking. These messages will serve as your school's community code so everyone learns to incorporate the philosophy into their lives. Our school's "BOOM 5" was created to focus on the attitude-gap made known by Baruti Kafele. We wanted our students to respect the hustle, love each other, work hard and not hardly work, follow through by saying what they mean and meaning what they say, get results, be self-reflective on their journeys, and lastly, the BOOM is to do it as their authentic selves.

- **Incorporate your academic philosophy into your students' learning**

Finally, you should also include your philosophy in your students' learning. You want your students to apply these values to their lives. One very effective way to do this is by taking the "3H Approach."

First, you "teach the head" by using academic facts and concepts to explain the philosophy and values. Make the teaching fun and engaging. Come up with fun, interactive ways to teach it. Second, you "guide the hand" by explaining how this philosophy relates to ordinary circumstances that happen in their lives, and how they can apply the philosophy when these situations happen. Role-playing and drama-filled theater are always great tools for the second phase. Third, you "touch the heart" by showing your students how this philosophy affects their lives and how applying it can give them a better understanding of what it truly means to be a valuable member of the community. This is where you bring people that look like them, or people they look up to, to spread the message. Reach out to influencers, celebrities, etc. You will be surprised at how many will hear you out if you attempt to contact them. I have brought many influencers to my school with the intent to reinforce our core values and philosophy at our school.

## Establishing Your School's Goals

A goal is a concept or idea of the future that you plan, envision, and work to achieve. For your school, coming up with goals that are effective is essential, especially if you want people to take notice. As a school leader, the goals you come up with should measure your effectiveness accurately. If you want to start an educational revolution, your goals should help you achieve this. To make things easier for you, here are a few suggestions to help you create effective goals:

- **Create a year-end goal**

    Create a year-end goal that you have envisioned for your school's future. Take note that I said 'goal'—singular. Pick one year-end goal that you think is a great investment for your school. This goal should sustain your focus over the year so that you can feel a unique sense of accomplishment when you finally achieve it. The year-end goal is very important, but it only becomes relevant if you make this goal a destination that is tangible for your staff. What I mean is, you should make the year-end goal like the super bowl, the Olympic gold medal, or Masters green jacket, if you love golf. As you present the year-end goal, you also present the tangible goal along with it. This strategy will give you direction towards a landmark destination. This will help build your movement, and after you present your goal, make sure you say, "LET'S BOOM!"

- **Create a foundational metric**

    As part of your goal-setting process, think of a foundational metric too. A foundational metric is a short-term goal that supports the school towards achieving the year end goal. These can also be highly motivating, as they are much easier to achieve, which means that you will always have reasons to celebrate. For instance, you can set a metric that you can accomplish within a couple of weeks or months. I always set a short-term metric for goals to be achieved either bi-weekly or once a month. Set goals for yourself, your teachers, your staff, and even your students. As you work together to reach your goals, you will suddenly create a structure and foundation for your revolution.

- **Make your goals 'SMART'**

SMART goals are the best types of goals, as they cover all the basic characteristics of these ideas for the future. SMART is an acronym that stands for:

- ○ **Specific:** When writing your goals down, add as many details as possible. Vague or unclear goals create confusion, and they might even make you lose motivation. But, when you have specific goals, you will know exactly what you need to do, and you will just do it!

- ○ **Measurable:** Find ways to measure the goals you create so that you know when you have already achieved them. For instance, when setting goals for your teachers, you can create a process to measure their performance in terms of understanding, practice, implementation success, or even satisfaction. You can do this through surveys, assessments, or demonstrations, for example.

- ○ **Achievable:** The goals you make should not be out of your reach. By now, you should already know yourself and the people around you more. You should know what you can do and what you cannot—yet. Think of goals that you know you can achieve right now. After you have overcome struggles and challenges, then you can choose to create more complex or difficult goals for the future.

○ **Realistic:** Aside from being achievable, make sure your goals are realistic too. Don't set goals that are too outrageous or impossible. Remember that you want to keep your motivation high and the best way to do this is to be as realistic as possible.

○ **Timely:** Finally, you should also set realistic timelines for your goals. This is an essential step. Without timelines, you won't feel motivated enough. You might end up pushing your goals back as you think of ways to distract yourself from them. Avoid this trap by including this final element of SMART goals.

In a perfect world, your goals would align with your district goals, however, they might not. As a leader, you must determine what the best is for your school community. Then clearly articulate your school's 'why' with regards to goal setting. By doing this, your district should support your school community. That way, all of your goals will still come together nicely and you will all work in harmony as you take the necessary steps to achieve your plans for the future.

## Take Time to Reflect

In this chapter, you have learned a wealth of information to help you set the stage for your revolutionary education journey. From creating your school's mission, vision, and values to thinking of your school's revolutionary mantra, and academic philosophy, then setting goals for the future, applying all the tips and tricks you have learned here will help you set the perfect stage for your school. Now, it's time to reflect on the following questions:

- Who do you seek to serve?

- What do you seek to accomplish?

- If your school is extremely successful over the next 3 to 5 years (thanks to your revolution), how will people describe your school?

- With this newfound success, how do you plan to proceed?

Much as you learned here, we are not done yet. Next, you need to focus on the people you work with—the ones who will help you make your school revolutionary!

# Chapter 6:

# Principle 2: Revolutionizing Staff Performance

*"But one of the things that we never discuss or we rarely discuss is the value and importance of human connection...relationships."* (Pierson)

After you have set the stage for the changes you plan to make in your school, the next thing to focus on is the people with whom you are working. Starting a revolution will be very difficult if you don't include your team in your plans. Creating a movement isn't about the positions you have, it is about the people you have. To make things easier for yourself, and to increase your chances of making amazing changes in your school, you must build a high-performing team—one that understands the vision, mission, philosophy, values, and goals of your school, and works collaboratively with you to achieve greatness.

As I have already shared, I was a coordinator first before I became a principal. When I held the title of 'coordinator', my mind was already working non-stop, as I was already planning to start an educational revolution. I would observe and process the situations happening around me, and then I imagined what I would do differently as a principal. Of course, this doesn't mean that you should start acting like the principal of your school if you don't hold that title yet. Instead, you should start developing a mindset of learning, while pushing yourself to have courageous conversations with others, as if you were already a school leader. That way, you don't end up becoming a leader who never planned to become one. If you really want to grow and prepare yourself to become the best leader you can be, you should already start now.

Now that I am the principal of my school, I have developed a framework to support leaders and educators by building a high-performance team. As a leader (no matter what organization or level), you must first be humble enough to put progress before your pride. You must also be hungry enough to find the hidden brilliance in each person at your school. And you must also be smart enough to know your boundaries and never overstep them. After you have this down, you must adopt the mantra, "To be is to have," which will most likely be a paradigm shift for you. This means that if you're aspiring for a leadership position (if you aren't in one yet), you have "to be" that leader first before you obtain the position.

This mantra doesn't just apply to being a leader. You will see this in all aspects of your life. You will see it with people who change their lifestyle habits, those who choose to focus on fitness, and those who learn how to manage their money better. In other words, you can become a millionaire in your mind and with actions, prior to earning your first million. In the same way, you can start revolutionizing your staff performance by applying this same process—and this is what you will be learning now.

## The Disciplines of Building a Healthy Team

One of the many people I have learned from in my life is the American writer, Patrick Lencioni. He specializes in business management books, and I love his ideas on team management. According to Lencioni, the basic character traits of an ideal team player are being humble, hungry, and smart. As a leader, I strove to be all these things because I wanted to become more than a leader—I also wanted to become a valuable team player.

When it comes to building a healthy, cohesive team, one of the most important things you should focus on is clarity. This clarity creates consistency throughout your team so that you can all work together towards your goals. You know that you have built a strong team when you don't have to deal with confusion, conflicts, or politics. Instead, you see high degrees of productivity, job satisfaction, and respect. Of course, creating this healthy, ideal team requires strategic planning and these essential disciplines:

## Cohesion and Leadership Village (Family) Atmosphere vs. Team Atmosphere

Building a family atmosphere is fundamentally different than building a team atmosphere. As a leader, I understood that this work is extremely difficult and the human element is hard to keep in a team atmosphere. Therefore, I believe you must focus on building a family. A family, can cry, laugh, yell, hug together and still be a family. A strong family atmosphere was the goal for me. For this, that means your leadership skills must come into play. It will be very difficult to work with a group of people if they have very different perceptions of what family is, in mind. This is why you should involve your staff (or at least key members of your staff) in the process of developing your school's vision, mission, and goals. Although you may have your own goals to improve your school, you will need the help of your teachers and staff to propel yourself—and your school—forward. As a leader, you must find ways to bring your team together by helping them understand the values of family and what they can potentially gain by supporting each other. If you can do this, you will make your team stronger by making them a united family.

## Clarity and Communication

After you have successfully improved your team's cohesiveness by building a family atmosphere, it's time to make things clearer for them. Gather your team and communicate your plans with them. Make sure that they all know what you are working toward and that they all understand their roles in the process. This step may take some time and effort, but you should consider this as your investment in the school. Each member of your team should be very clear on why they are in the school, what they should do, how they should act, what their priorities are, and how you will all work together to find success. To bring clarity to your team, you must learn how to communicate with them effectively.

## Reinforcement and Encouragement

After you have united your team and clarified your goals, you can maintain the health of your team through constant encouragement and reinforcement. If needed, remind them of everything you have agreed upon, and always try to keep an atmosphere of positivity in your school. Your team should be able to approach you openly and talk to you about any issues that are happening within your school. This is the most effective way for you to stay on top of things. As long as your team knows that they can communicate with you openly and that they always have your support, you can continue working with a healthy team that is driven to succeed.

## The Value of Relationships in Education

Relationships are very personal things. As a leader, I personally value each and every relationship that I have. As Baruti Kafele, one of the most inspiring educators I know, once said, "How can a leader even imagine moving a school forward without first demonstrating genuine gratitude for all that teachers do?" This is a powerful question that carries a lot of insight. When I heard him utter these words, I realized how true they were and how significant they are, especially if you're trying to revolutionize the performance of the people with whom you work.

In education, relationships are key. Let me repeat that. In education, relationships are key! As a school leader, there is something I call the micro-unit of change, which is the positive relational impact of leaders to teachers, teachers to students, and students to outcomes. In other words, the leader, or principal, needs to have good relationships with teachers. Teachers need to have good relationships with their colleagues. They also need to have good relationships with their students and the parents of their students. Staff members need to have good relationships with the teachers, parents, and students as well. School leaders, of course, need to maintain good relationships with virtually everyone in the school. When this happens, you essentially create the "happy wife, happy life, happy house, happy spouse" atmosphere on campus. The impact behind this intent is that happy teachers will create happy students, and happy students will then reach for their dreams. Students reaching for their dreams will cycle back to good data, which makes for a happy principal— BOOM! Rita Pierson, the inspiring professional educator, once said that every child deserves a champion. In her exact words, "Every child deserves a champion; an adult who will never give up on them, who understands the power of connection, and insists that they become the best they can possibly be." But what does this mean? It might sound silly to some people, but as the leader of your school, you have to be that champion. While inspiring other champions, let me explain what this means through the following points:

- You must become a champion for all of your staff members and all of your students. You must be just that—a champion for ALL of them. Don't just be the champion for the staff and students who are driven to learn, are likable, and have a positive outlook on the school. You should also be the champion of the most resistant, difficult, and challenging staff and students. This will take a lot of effort, patience, and planning, but you can do this by learning how to build rapport and establish relationships with them.

- Relationships are important drivers for human learning. When human beings see that you are genuinely trying to reach out to them, this can be a powerful intrinsic motivator for them. This, in turn, teaches them to be self-motivated. They will always stay hungry because they know that they have a champion rooting for them—and that champion is you.

- While it is important to be your school's overall champion, you should also be aware that this role will take a toll on you as a leader. You will have to work harder to find ways to take care of yourself. As mentioned before, this revolution is not going to be easy. It comes with heavy loads. But it is important to identify the workload and prepare for it. As a lead champion of your school, self-care is important.

Being a champion involves establishing genuine relationships with your students. But, you should also focus on building strong relationships with your staff and teachers too. Let me share an example with you. At our school, I have regular one-on-one meetings with my teachers and staff members to strengthen my relationships with them. During these meetings, I ask questions like: "What are you looking for in a principal?" or "How might I best support you on your mission this year?" As a principal, asking such questions show that I am willing to "set the stage" by helping my teachers and staff. In turn, it becomes easier for them to make the magic happen.

When the people around you know that there is at least one person who believes in them and challenges them, they will feel a strong urge to become the best versions of themselves. And when that person is the same person who leads the whole school, their motivation becomes even stronger. As simple as relationships might seem, they truly play an essential role in the world of education.

# The Secret of Attracting and Retaining Quality Teachers

The teachers and staff in your school play a huge role in its success. Therefore, you must learn how to hire well. As you search for the best team of individuals, you must remember that you are searching for someone who is humble, hungry, and smart throughout the process. Yes, it's important to hire individuals who can perform well, as they can potentially drive your school forward. But you must also learn how to find people who will fit into your school well. Think about it: if you hire a person who seems like a great fit (because they have a wonderful personality, or for some other reason) but you know that they won't perform well, this won't be ideal. Similarly, if you find someone who is assertive and hungry for success but doesn't share the same ideals and values as those of you and your school, such a person wouldn't be ideal either. You must find people who have a good balance of performance, as well as the right fit for your school. This will make it much easier for you and everyone else to work with the people you hire.

If you already have an amazing team to work with, good for you! You want to have a team of people who will stay with your school through thick and thin, people who will go through challenges with you and celebrate successes with you too. If you feel like you don't have enough of these types of people in your school, then you must learn how to attract and retain quality teachers and staff. To do this, here are some tips:

- **Come up with a rigorous recruitment process**

    To find the best people for your school, you must have the right process in place. If your recruitment process is too easy, you might end up with people who can't keep up with what you're trying to achieve. Therefore, you should come up with a rigorous recruitment process to screen your candidates and hire the most passionate and motivated ones.

- **Creatively compensate**

  Educators across the nation are severely underpaid for the work they do and the value they bring. Therefore, as much as you want to believe that goals and ambitions are enough to keep quality people around, you must accept the reality. For most people, compensation is one of the most important aspects of employment. If you want the best people in your school, you must be willing to compensate them well, too. Offer a competitive salary to your teachers and staff, and always make sure that you compensate them in a timely manner–always. You must be creative and intentional with your budget for your teachers. Support your staff by paying them for their time, and your return on your investment will explode.

- **Provide meaningful support and evaluation**

  Finally, you should also provide your teachers and staff with meaningful, genuine support. Continuously evaluate the members of your team and provide them with feedback as needed. This shows that you support their growth. Also, provide them with opportunities to move forward in their careers by offering plenty of opportunities for professional development. By doing this, your teachers and staff will see that they have a future in your school, which means that they will stick around and even help you make the changes you want to implement for the betterment of your school.

## The Best Ways of Maximizing Staff Performance

In the world of education, staff development is essential. All members of a school's team play important roles, and if everyone performs at their best, your school will run like clockwork. Therefore, you must find ways to maximize your staff performance to ensure that your school will move toward the future you have always envisioned. The progress of your organization depends on the extent to which your staff is positively developed and motivated. This simply means that moving forward will be much easier if the people around you are highly motivated and have a positive outlook.

The importance of staff development cannot be emphasized enough. This will help align personal needs and organizational roles toward your main goal of developing thought processes and behaviors that work in harmony with the organizational purposes you have shared, and with your staff's own self-fulfillment. As I mentioned in the beginning of this chapter, I developed a framework of support for teachers and educators.

This framework helped me build a high-performing team, and it starts by performing a team audit. This team audit can be broken down into three major components (RSL):

- **Results**

  By thinking about the results you want, you will also be giving your team a clear vision. Then, you can start peeling back the layers to identify your team's end-goal. The results should embody your team's goals and culture.

- **Skills**

  To get the results you are seeking, you must know the skills you need. Think of it this way: If you order a product from IKEA that requires assembly, you need to get all the parts you need. However, if you know nothing about the product and how to assemble it, you might end up purchasing more or less than you need to put it together. In the same way, you need to know what skills are required so that you can work toward getting results without delay.

- **Leverage**

   After knowing what skills you need, you must start building relationships with the members of your team. This helps you find out who possesses the skills you are looking for, so that you can leverage those skills. This is something I always advise educators and school leaders to do. When I ask educators if they believe that each student has a talent or brilliance hidden within them, they always answer yes. If so, doesn't this mean that each teacher and staff member also has a hidden talent or brilliance? Yes, of course! Therefore, the key to building your high-performance team is to identify the hidden skills within each of your teachers and staff members, and then leverage these to meet your vision and achieve your results.

   By focusing on these results and the strengths of your team, you can encourage self-development from a more positive point of view. When the individual dispositions of your staff members are congruent with the growth you expect to happen, then there is a higher likelihood that things will fall into place. When it comes to maximizing staff development, here are some things to remember:

- When thinking of development processes, focus on the interests and strengths of your staff and teachers.

- Have a conversation to clarify your expectations, your staff's expectations, and which aspects of staff development are non-negotiable. Clarifying these things improves accountability across the board.

- Provide opportunities for personal and professional development, such as mentoring, peer-assisted leadership, and coaching, for example.

- By creating a systematic process of staff development, this will foster trust, motivation, and higher levels of staff investment.

- Create an evaluation process that informs your staff about their performance levels. Communicating this promptly and directly makes everything clearer and easier for everyone. These reviews and evaluations make your team members aware of what they are doing well and what they need to improve to become more valuable members of the team.

Whenever possible, celebrate your team members for the progress they make and the accomplishments they achieve towards your school's goals. By doing all these things, you can maximize staff performance while encouraging them to feel more invested in your school's vision. When this happens, you will notice that the resistors and blockers in your school have limited impact.

## The Importance of School Team Awareness

Another way for you to improve the cohesiveness of your team is to get to know each of them better. Increasing your school team awareness can be done by knowing how the people in your team relate to and work with others. Personally, I believe that one very effective way to do this is by learning your team's love languages. Specifically, Dr. Gary Chapman's *The 5 Love Languages* is a powerful way to get to know your team. Knowing these enhances your ability to connect with your team, increase positivity, and help them feel more appreciated. Here are some ways to increase your awareness and apply love languages in the workplace:

- **Acts of service** can come in the form of helping the members of your team accomplish a task or even volunteering to collaborate with them to complete projects.

- **Gift-giving** can come in the form of giving simple yet high-value gifts to the members of your team. This can come in the form of material things, but it can also come in the form of additional rest days with pay (if your school can afford it).

- **Physical touch** can come in the form of fun things like handshakes, high-fives, and fist-bumps. This love language is one of the trickier ones, since some people don't appreciate physical touch, especially in the workplace. So it's up to you to determine what's appropriate.

- **Quality time** can come in the form of spending time with the members of your team even outside of the workplace. For instance, you can set school outings or team building activities wherein you can all spend quality time together, while having fun.

- **Words of affirmation** is the easiest love language to express, as long as you express these words genuinely. Simple words of appreciation can go a long way, and they cost nothing!

To determine the love languages of your team members, you can perform self-assessments to learn more about them, their strengths, and their potential areas of growth.

## Take Time to Reflect

Some of the greatest treasures you have in your school are the people with whom you work. This is why the second step in starting your revolution is focused on your teachers and staff. Now that you have gained insight on how to revolutionize staff performance, it's time to reflect. Here are some questions for you to ponder before you move on to the next chapter:

- Right now, how much do you know about your individual teachers and staff?

- What is the most important contribution each of them makes to your school?

- How can you inspire your teachers and staff to improve their performance?

- How do you show appreciation to your team members? Do you think you can improve your current methods?

- How can you improve relationships among teachers and staff members?

- How can you improve relationships between teachers and students?

- What are the ways for you to reach out to the students in your school even if you don't teach them directly?

# Chapter 7:

# Principle 3: Building a Restorative School

*"The greatness of a community is most accurately measured by the compassionate actions of its members."* (Scott-King)

The next thing to work on is creating a Restorative School by focusing on restorative practices. The root of the word 'restorative' is 'restore,' which means to repair, or bring something back to its former glory. If you have already built something great, but things have deteriorated over time, then you need restorative practices to make things better. Take relationships, for instance. If you have already built relationships with the people in your school, but you have somehow let these relationships weaken, now is the time to repair those relationships.

During one of the many presentations I have done, I will never forget the time when a school principal from New Jersey approached me after my speech. She said that my voice embodies the 'LOVE' that she spreads to her students. Then she continued by explaining what LOVE meant—Living **O**ff **V**illage **E**nergy. As simple as this comment might have been for her, it made a huge impact on me. I even adopted it in my school to LOVE meaning-Learning **O**ff **V**illage **E**nergy. Restorative practices must be part of your school's fluid philosophy to make it easier for you to apply these practices whenever you feel like there is a need to do so. An essential part of restorative practices will be first understanding your school community and environment, then building your school community and environment, then restoring your school community and environment.

## School Environmental Scan

By definition, an environmental scan is the continuous monitoring of occurrences and trends in the environment of an organization, both external and internal. Therefore, a school environmental scan involves constantly keeping track of anything that happens in your school that has an effect on current and future success. The results that you obtain from your school environmental scan will be very useful in planning strategies and building your community.

When conducting a school environmental scan, consider all internal measures, like trauma, programs, suspensions, suicidal ideations, budget deficits, community involvement opportunities or events, and leadership changes, as well as external events, including academic interests, demographics, economies, labor market, philanthropy, politics, public policies, research, and technology. An effective environmental scan allows you to understand qualitative and quantitative changes in your school. By performing this scan, you can come up with a number of significant environmental indicators that have the most significant effect on the community you are trying to build in your school.

## Trauma Informed

*In high school I learned chemistry, biology, But not how to cope with anxiety, Or how I could feel like I'm by myself on an island With depression on all sides of me.* (Big Sean)

As you prepare to build a Restorative school, it is important you acknowledge the trauma that exists. The first thing any school should do prior to beginning their path towards restorative practices is to understand, recognize, and respond to the historical, trans-generational, and current traumas that exist in your school community. This means, as the school leader or teacher, you must dive deep to truly know your community, to be prepared to respond. I compare this to a real estate developer that has to design a safe house in Florida and California. In order to build the two homes, the developer must understand the factors that exist, such as hurricanes in Florida, and earthquakes in California. The understanding of this allows the developer to then recognize that the plans for both need to be structurally different from each other to support the environmental factors. Because the developer recognized the needs, she or he can now respond by developing, planning, and executing a safe and successful plan that accommodates each potential homeowner. That is essentially what each school and classroom must do; however, what I have found is that many schools understand that trauma exists, and even implement a workshop or two to recognize trauma, but then fail to respond to trauma.

In order to lead with equity a school must be trauma informed. As a leader this also means that you consider the vicarious trauma that exists with your staff. The application of **U.R.R.**-**U**nderstanding, **R**ecognizing, and **R**esponding to trauma has to be a foundational principle that is implemented with fidelity and intentionality with the entire school community. In order to properly respond to trauma, you must continue what I call the cycle of breakthrough, to sustain a community of collective healing. This framework leads you to Maslow before Bloom.

## Maslow Before Bloom

Before we dive into restorative practices, let's take a look at human nature. As the leader of a school, you should never allow your school to lose the value of humanity. Every time you plan to make decisions or revolutionary changes, you should always consider every other person in your school. In other words, decisions should be human-centered.

Have you ever heard the phrase, "Maslow before Bloom"? Basically, this means that human beings need to meet their basic needs first before they can embrace academic learning. Abraham Maslow is famous for his "Hierarchy of Needs," which include belonging, esteem, physiological, safety, and self-actualization. These are the basic needs of human beings that we all strive to meet in our lives.

Benjamin Bloom, on the other hand, is famous for his "Taxonomy of Educational Objectives," which include cognitive tiers known as analysis, application, comprehension, evaluation, knowledge, and synthesis. As you can see, the needs presented by Maslow are much more basic than the ones presented by Bloom. Although all of these are important, you cannot focus on the educational needs (objectives) until you make sure that you meet the basic needs of your teachers, staff, and, yes, students.

It's that simple!

As an educator, I encourage you to reflect on the relationships you have established with the people in your school. Reflect on what you do for them, and then ask yourself if you are helping them meet their most basic needs. If you notice that some people—teachers, staff members, or students—are struggling, they might need some extra attention. Here are some ways you can make things easier for the people around you so that they can go beyond the needs described by Maslow, and start focusing on the ones described by Bloom:

- Greet everyone warmly, genuinely, and with eye-contact. This will help people feel like they belong and are accepted in your school.

- Always show respect to everyone. If you have done something out of line, whether intentional or not, apologize. If someone makes a mistake, forgive them. If you notice anyone struggling or feeling unhappy, approach them, and communicate. All of these will help improve the self-esteem of the people around you.

- Promote the health and well-being of the people in your school by providing time for mental health, incorporating exercises and physical activity in their schedules, and even set rest and mental health days once in a while. Yes, promoting that your staff take a mental health day is important. Such provisions will help meet the physiological needs of your teachers, staff, and students.

- Model expectations of your school and provide everyone with opportunities to practice things like yoga, mindfulness, and other self-care fulfillments. At my school, we had yoga during planning time that we paid for. Yes, I paid my teachers to participate in yoga to connect by disconnecting. Things like this help in different ways. As the team sees that you are not just talking about it, but you are doing something about it, you will see monumental shifts in your school. Just remember to be consistent and non-judgmental. This will help everyone feel safe in your school.

By doing all these things (and anything else you can think of), you will raise your people up. You will help them feel happier in your school and more willing to start working on the educational objectives you have envisioned.

## PBIS Framework

Positive Behavioral Interventions and Supports (PBIS) is a framework with three tiers based on evidence. It is meant to integrate and improve all the practices, systems, and data that affect the outcomes of students each day. By applying PBIS to your school, you can propel your students forward and increase the likelihood of their success.

The main purpose of PBIS is to enhance the overall equity, effectiveness, and efficiency of your school. For your students, PBIS improves their academic, emotional, and social outcomes—even for students from underrepresented groups and those with disabilities. To help you understand PBIS and come up with a plan for how to apply it in your school, let's go through the three tiers of this framework:

## Tier 1: Providing Regular, Proactive Support to All Students

This tier provides support to all the students in your school. You would teach targeted expectations and acknowledge those who practice these expectations. Here, you will:

- Introduce targeted expectations to all of your students. These are school-wide expectations that everyone agrees to pursue.

- The key to implementing a successful PBIS at your school is prevention, not intervention. However, you want to create a comprehensive identification of an additional staff-to-student love program at your school.

- Monitor the progress of your students regularly.

- Gather data to use whenever there is a need to make decisions in terms of student expectations.

For this tier, you can create a team to help you come up with the strategies and implement them. You may also enlist the help of classroom teachers, parents, and student leaders. Before you can start implementing the practices for the next two tiers, these practices should already be in place. That way, you can identify the students to focus on in the next tier.

## Tier 2: Providing Additional Support for At-Hope Students

The final step of the first tier will help you determine who are the "high-risk" students. These students will require additional love and support from you to prevent them from developing a resentment problem towards school. It is critical that this tier focuses on finding out the hidden treasure in the students. Here, you will:

- Instead of pinpointing the behavior problem, you will pinpoint the student's value and strengths.

- Instead of just implementing the usual targeted interventions such as behavioral support, academic support, social skills groups, and self-management groups, focus on the students' creative and practical intelligence. Peel back the layers to level-up on connectors for the students that reinforce their sense of belonging. Interventions like this are more student-centered but must be available continuously, must be function-based, constantly monitored, and not manipulated.

The practices in this tier are more difficult to implement, but the rewards are also greater. It is critical for schools to review their PBIS framework to determine if they are reinforcing harmful strategies for students by forcing students to come to school to "sit down, shut up, and color between the lines." A framework that reinforces this behavior is a system that deserves rethinking. You need to have a separate team to implement these practices, along with the students' classroom teachers, and a behavior specialist. Be creative and enjoy finding the hidden treasures of your students.

## *Tier 3: Providing Intensive Individualized Support to Targeted Students*

After implementing the practices for the second-tier support, you may still have a few students who require more love. This targeted group of students is composed of those who cannot or would not connect with your previous efforts. Often, students here may have more challenging and complex situations. When you reach this tier, you will:

- Identify the students who need intensive and individualized support based on the assessments you have done in tier 2.

- Evaluate each student to determine their individual needs.

- Ensure that all the targeted students are equitably and fully supported by your school by maximizing your resources and implementing the right strategies.

- You take them under your wing. Yes, you as the Principal, the leader, should create a program to love, mentor, teach, and reteach the students in this tier. As the Principal, I take pride in making an impact with my students, therefore, if I have students who are struggling to connect in the school community, I see it as my obligation as the school leader to be held accountable for the students' connection to the environment.

- Continuously monitor each student's progress to determine the effectiveness of your practices.

When working with students in this tier, you have to consider the context and culture of each student. At my school, we created a Very Important Pupil List or "VIP List" that I adopted from a great Principal named Jose Navarro. The VIP List is a profile of each student that aligns the love language and the essential skills—such as grit, growth mindset, and emotional regulation—for each student. This VIP List provides us with robust information for each student to determine if our supports have been effective. In order to do this, a great resource we use is a survey platform called Panorama Education. By doing this, we've learned more about our students through their local environments, personal characteristics, and learning histories. You will also have to align more support staff, as this tier will need more love. Consider including specialists such as coaches, counselors, and therapists.

## Restorative Practices

We are finally here to now "restore" our school community. This approach to discipline which moves away from punishment, and toward restoring a sense of love, connection, and well-being for all those affected by a harmful act is important and can't be ignored. It provides the entire school community with a way to ensure accountability, while at the same time, breaking the school to prison pipeline. If implemented with fidelity, this approach acknowledges everyone and makes everybody feel like somebody. It brings attention that, when a person does harm, it affects the persons they hurt, the community, and themselves. When we use restorative practices, we are making the attempt to leverage our village(school) to repair the harm caused by one person to another, and to the community, so that the village is moved toward healing. Here are some benefits of implementing these restorative practices in your school:

- A restorative approach in a school empowers students to think about themselves and how they deal with one another. They learn to work on developing healthy relationships and managing conflict. Implementing a restorative approach in a school creates the "it takes a village" atmosphere.

- When restorative practices are implemented with intent and applied within a school, they improve the school climate, promote community, and reduce student conflicts. At all of my schools, we implemented a school-wide community building hour to support our community. The curriculum was developed by a community team and was implemented by our staff with fidelity.

- Restorative practices work to lower suspension and expulsion rates, and to build an aspirational school environment with the goal of eliminating racially disproportionate discipline practices.

With all these benefits to look forward to, the next thing to think about is how to apply restorative practices. Here are some suggestions for you to start with:

- Conduct Community Circles. These focus on building strong, genuine relationships with your school community and your students to promote positivity in the different aspects of your school environment.

- Provide ongoing professional development for your teachers to improve their relationship building skills. Also, provide them with continuous support and coaching as needed— building relationships isn't easy.

- Introduce a reward framework to your teachers and staff so that you can come up with a plan for how to implement it together.

- Identify the pioneers who are interested in helping you implement this reward framework. Rewarding your students is a must.

- Start implementing a reward framework to target the expectations of students throughout the school.

- Determine the capacity of your school to take on this set of practices that will potentially create a shift in your culture. As you do this, consider the commitment and resources needed to ensure success.

- Add staff members, parents, and student leaders to the implementation of a reward system, PBIS, and restorative practices.

- Establish practices that allow students to lead this work to take it to another level.

- Use the affective language to engage your students in self-reflection and emotional connection, especially when issues or conflicts arise.

- Focus on becoming a school that has an amazing environment to restore back to.

The fact is, PBIS and restorative practices complement each other. The PBIS system will help you create and evaluate positive outcomes, in terms of behaviors, while restorative practices will provide you with the tools you need to create those positive outcomes. Together, you can use these to provide consistent, clear expectations and routines that will help you reach your goal of creating better functioning classrooms and a more positive school community, a true village.

## Applying Restorative Practices in Your School

The key to restorative practices is that a school shift away from thinking about "laws being broken, who broke the law, and how we punish the people who broke the laws". Instead, it requires us to explore that there was harm caused in the village (school), there's a disagreement or dispute, there's conflict, and how do we repair the harm, address the conflict, and meet the needs so that relationships and the community can be repaired and restored. It's a different orientation. It is a shift. Take a look at this table to see the differences:

| Traditional Approach | Restorative Approach |
|---|---|
| School and rules violated | People and relationships violated |
| Approach that focuses on establishing guilt | Approach that identifies needs and expectations |
| Accountability = punishment | Accountability = understanding impact |
| Person who experienced harm is ignored | Person who experienced harm is involved in the healing process |

Restorative practices will enable you to make your school better than it is now. By applying such practices, you will focus on building relationships by communicating and supporting students. While following the PBIS tiers, you may want to apply the following restorative practices too:

- **Transform Policy**

  If you have not noticed I strongly believe language matters, therefore it is important to transform your language in all policies around discipline. We changed our School Discipline Policy, to our Restorative Policy. Right now, think about the existing discipline practices in your school for dealing with challenging situations. To help with your reflection, here are some questions to ask yourself:

- Does your current discipline policy have punitive language? Does your school go beyond focusing solely on policy violations? (What's under the surface of your students?)

- Does the accountability for student behavior focus on reinforcing the expectations?

- Is there equal concern being given to harm experienced by individuals and the community?

- What role does the external community have with the policy?

- Have support people such as an advocate, mentor, or other person deemed appropriate (given the circumstances) been identified, approved by, and provided for each person involved?

- Are your policies effective to the most challenging students?

- Does your school have an accountability of praise that equals or surpasses your student consequences?

Often, schools use other disciplinary methods when dealing with what they deem as problematic behaviors, especially if those behaviors are from black students. Therefore, it is critical to set a standard for how the school will address challenges and harm to the community.

Take, for instance, punitive (traditional) discipline. Here, "unwanted behaviors" are defined as a student's choice to deviate from expected behaviors or break the rules of the school. Teachers establish guilt and dispense punishment, most of which can cause harm to the student. This type of discipline often involves stigmatizing or shaming students as part of the disciplinary actions. Another example is the zero-tolerance method. For this, discipline typically comes in the form of suspension, expulsion, or referring the student to other schools. Although the goal of this method is to make the school safer for everyone, the disciplinary methods used are often extreme even if the "violations" aren't that outrageous. It is time to break the adopted Prison Warden structure that exists in our schools.

You cannot possibly establish relationships nor call yourself a Revolutionary Educator when using these types of methods. Some people might believe that they work, but if you want to restore your school to make it better than it has ever been, you need to come up with a plan to do so—a plan that involves the right practices.

- **Build a team to help you out**

  When creating the team that will help you implement PBIS and restorative practices, choose people who believe in what you want to achieve. Select those who are interested in learning all about these practices so that they can apply everything appropriately. You may have to implement the RSL-Team Audit, to process and determine who shines at conflict resolution, relationship-building, and those who can effectively work with building the type of village the community needs.

- **Practice inclusion when determining possible consequences and accountabilities**

  Many people think that restorative practices mean no accountability for misbehavior, but that is wrong. However, what many educators are really saying is that there isn't an instant punitive satisfaction they receive, which is totally different. When it's time to talk about the consequences of challenging behaviors, including teachers, staff, and even students in the discussion can be highly beneficial. This awakens a powerful sense of accountability, especially among students. Of course, you would have to plan such an encounter well so that you can pull it off effectively and get the results for which you're aiming.

- **Model the empathetic and compassionate qualities you want to promote**

Although explaining your expectations will help everyone understand, modeling these expectations will help drive your point home. As other people see that you are "practicing what you preach", they will feel more inspired to do the same. The good news is, if you really believe in these behaviors, modeling them will be very easy.

- **Communicate when faced with conflict**

  Finally, when faced with conflict, respond by communicating. When you notice an inappropriate behavior, start a conversation about it. This allows you to understand the context of the situation and the reasons why it happened in such a way. Communication will help you prevent conflicts from getting worse or being blown out of proportion.

  These strategies are fairly simple, but the impact they will make at your school will be great. Therefore, the sooner you can start practicing them, the better.

## Meetings to Support Your Restorative Practices

Your plans for implementing restorative practices are slowly falling into place. Now, it's time to come up with a plan for when you will meet with your team to discuss strategies, implementation, and evaluation. The frequency of these meetings will depend on the participants. Also, you don't have to facilitate the meetings all the time. You can set meetings wherein teachers, school administrators, or even school counselors will be the ones to lead. It is essential that you embed subtle practices in your meetings that reinforce your plans such as beginning these meetings with a community-building activity, checking in and out with your staff, or using a talking piece at your meetings from time to time. When creating your schedule for meetings, it can look like this:

| Types of Teams | Frequency | Participants |
|---|---|---|
| **Administrative Leadership Team** | Once a week | Principal, Vice Principal |
| **Grade Level Teams** | Once every two weeks | Principal, Grade Level Teachers, Social Workers |
| **Equity Leadership Team** | Once every two weeks | Principal, Vice Principal, Coaches/ Coordinators/ Department Heads, Community Members, Students, Parents |
| **Student Support Team** | Once every month | Student Leaders, Parent Leaders, Special Education Teachers, Behavioral Specialists |

## Take Time to Reflect

Everything that I have shared with you in this chapter comes from my own experiences in the field of education. During my time as a restorative justice advisor– and this was early in my mission–I was tasked to decrease the number of dropouts, fights, referrals, defiant acts, suspensions, and expulsions for boys of color at the middle school I worked. Like many African American educators who connect with students, they expected me to be the "discipline guy"— the black student savior of sorts.

While I welcomed the challenge, it was, and still is, a critical problem within a system that stereotypes black men in education as glorified security officers. I was the restorative discipline guy, the guy everyone called to save the day. Imagine being the point person and tasked with restoring a school that really didn't value the village approach around addressing the needs of every student. Imagine that while the school location is placed at the epicenter of several rival gang communities, this made things extremely challenging. The mission I had was to develop a "Program for Restoring Positive Self".

Try to envision middle-school boys of color while transforming the language of "at-risk" boys to "at-hope" young men. As challenging as this was, I successfully created a program with a local law enforcement officer named Keith Linton, which we called, "Boys to Gentlemen." Through this program, we created a safe place for young boys to feel like they belong and can connect with others. Through this program, I was able to accomplish the task set before me. I faced a lot of challenges and overcame numerous obstacles. When I implemented restorative practices correctly, things got better. And although the program was successful, in order for this program to be sustainable and scalable it needed to be invested in by the collective school. A school that lacks collective involvement and investment from administration is a program that typically fades when the facilitator departs.

I hope my short anecdote makes you feel inspired. And as you process the journey I went through, along with everything you have learned in this chapter, here are some questions to ask yourself:

- How do you create a systemic approach that is restorative? Is it one that is filled with repair and love instead of punitive and destructive methods?

- What challenges are your students facing right now that you can address with restorative practices?

- What do you hope to accomplish with your regular meetings?

# Chapter 8:

# Principle 3: Revolutionizing Your School Culture

*"Probably the most important and most difficult job of the school leader is to change the prevailing culture...ultimately a school's culture has far more influence on life and learning in the school than the state department of education, the superintendent, the school board, or even the principal can ever have." (Barth)*

As a revolutionary leader, one of the most important things you can do for your school is to revolutionize its culture. You must learn how to transform your school into an environment where your students feel secure because they know that the entire school staff has their best interests at heart. As a revolutionary principal, I have experienced revolutionizing cultures in different schools. But to get you set in this chapter, let me share one of the most significant changes I made which was the creation of a Culturally Relevant House System.

The School House System is much like the one in the famous *Harry Potter* books, and it was popularized by The Ron Clark Academy in Atlanta. I was introduced to the house system through Harry Potter, but I really connected with it when I observed the use of the house system on Instagram by The Ron Clark Academy. To give you a quick summary, Hogwarts (the wizarding school in the *Harry Potter* books) is divided into four houses, named after the last name of each founder: Godric Gryffindor, Salazar Slytherin, Rowena Ravenclaw, and Helga Hufflepuff.

The Ron Clark Academy coined its own House System with the name "Altruismo," which has its origins in the rainforests of the

Amazon. There, a group of powerful Brazilians received this name because of its meaning in Portuguese, the "givers". Amistad is the House that originates from Spain. This group consists of a group of quiet but powerful students who are known most for their kindness of heart. Because of this, their name means "friendship" in the language of their ancestry. Isibindi is the house that consists of a tight-knit group of students who, like a pride of African lions, consider family as the most important thing. In Zulu, the term "Isibindi" means courage. The last house is Rêveur, a royal House with a French name that means "idealists" or "dreamers". Very interesting, right?

After my observation, I came up with a way to bring more of an impact to cultivate our culturally relevant school community. I came up with our own House System that sought to focus on the following:

- Friendship, because of the love and respect we want our young people to have for each other. We also wanted to decrease the instances of bullying at our school.

- Advocacy, because we wanted our students to gain sacred knowledge so they can speak up and speak out.

- Courage, because we wanted our students to stand for something so they won't fall for anything.

- Motivation, because we wanted our students to develop intrinsic motivation, one of the most powerful things that promote the BOOM effect.

After determining the core characteristics we wanted to focus on, we then sought to name our houses after individuals with whom our school community can connect. I worked with a team for this. We had brainstorming sessions and came up with some amazing names for our houses:

- We named the house of friendship, "Team Mobama," after the former First Lady of the United States, Michelle Obama

- We named the house of courage, "Team KAP," after the American activist, Colin Kaepernick

- We named the house of advocacy, "Team AOC," after US Representative, Alexandria Ocasio Cortez

- We named the house of motivation, "Team Hussle," after the late and great American rapper, Nipsey Hussle

Because of our effective use of social media to spread the word about our school (more on this later), I encountered a middle school teacher, Alexis Moorer, who felt inspired by this house system we had developed. This culturally relevant house system moved her, and she wanted to try it with her class. To do this, she adopted her own house system using The House of Achievement (named after Lebron James), The House of Advocacy (named after Alexandria Ocasio-Cortez), The House of Justice (named after Sonia Sotomayor), and The House of Friendship (named after Barack Obama). She divided her class of 40 students into groups of ten and started to transform her class using this revolutionary (and fun!) idea.

As simple as creating house systems might seem to other people, it has the potential to become a true game-changer if you can implement it correctly. By implementing house systems, you can emphasize the importance and sense of belonging that all students need. It has been so effective that it has transformed many educators and classrooms across the nation. Furthermore, this house system created an opportunity to gamify our students' learning. We created constructive enrichment and academic activities for each of the teams to compete with each other while developing a sense of belonging. Students compete with grades, attendance, civic responsibility, sports, and more. Basically, anything we can think of, we gamify it for our students and this makes things more magical.

Because of this, we call our school, "The Happiest place in South Central Los Angeles, California".

## Starting the Revolution

Creating a house system at your school accompanied with restorative practices are essential in revolutionizing your school's culture. These practices promote strong, healthy relationships, enabling you to build a healthy community of educators and students. Part of implementing restorative practices is to use restorative language. To do this, you have to empower your teachers and students that the power of restorative language is about expression. This allows them to approach situations in a calmer, more rational way. This also promotes thinking, listening, and dealing with issues cooperatively. If you provide the language your teachers and students need to promote the culture you are trying to create, this will enhance your restorative and revolutionary efforts.

Asking the right questions and using the proper language throughout the school will ease your transition into a revolutionary culture. Teachers, staff, and students must learn this language to ensure that everyone in the school is communicating the right way. For instance, if something happened that involved a conflict between students, instead of shaming or blaming the students involved in the incident, you would ask questions like:

- What happened?

- How were you feeling when it happened?

- What was on your mind when it happened?

- Aside from yourself, who else was affected by this incident? How were they affected?

- What do you need to do to make things right?

- How can we address your needs together?

- How do you think you and everyone else affected can move on? The main thing about restorative language is that it doesn't focus on criticism, judgment, or blame. Instead, it focuses on the present, the people involved, and how to use restorative practices when dealing with conflicts. The more you practice using such language, the more natural it becomes. To do this, you should encourage the use of restorative language in classrooms, meetings, and even in the hallways—not just in formal settings. Here are some ways to encourage this:

- Have productive and enlightening conversations with all the educators in your school about the importance of restorative language and how to use it when interacting with students.

- Encourage the leaders of your school to be about it and not just talk about it. They should be the ones who use such language consistently no matter who they communicate with.

- Post signs and posters throughout your school that encourage the use of restorative language.

When it comes to improving your school climate and culture, you must focus on restorative practices and preventative measures instead of reactive behaviors. This will take a lot of time and practice to master, which is why you should encourage everyone to be invested so that consistency is ensured.

## Creating a Revolutionary Atmosphere

*"I've learned that people will forget what you said, people will forget what you did, but people will never forget how you made them feel."* (Angelou).

When I was still in school, I was the kid who was completely disconnected. Although I came from a family of educators, I couldn't see the relevance of what I was learning to how it was going to change my circumstances. Once, I even had a 1.8 GPA in high school because I was fed up with what I was learning. However, when I became a principal, I wanted to build a high school I wish I attended, a school that could connect with every student's interest. To do this, we moved with a connection of what students seek to discover. Self-discovery accompanied with cultural discovery are two critical components of finding one's purpose. This ideology had us learn more about the interest and needs of our students which forced us to create a music studio, a design lab, and even a one-on-one robot program for students who want to learn how to code. We had students passionate about fashion so we purchased a heat-press with programs for students to design their own shirts. By being intentional about this, it makes every student feel like somebody.

Through observation, we knew that our students loved music. To build an aspirational environment for them, we established a partnership with Stix, a local rap artist and activist, then produced a school theme song to help our students feel connected. The song is entitled, "Let's BOOM", and you can find it on all streaming platforms. We also transformed the standard "Uniform Policy" to an apparel line by establishing a partnership with a clothing company called Baller Bellys. They loved our message so much that they agreed to design apparel for our students that was diverse and made everyone feel good. Fashion is a form of expression and I have always been against a very strict "uniform policy" that is not diverse with the uniqueness of every child. I believe if more schools adopted an expanded apparel line that was more inclusive it will allow more students to be themselves. Like Deion Sanders said, "If you look good, you feel good, if you feel good, you play good, if you play good, they pay good." This same concept applies with students; if they look good, they feel good, if they feel good, they work harder, and if they work harder, they get better results.

These are just some examples of how to create a friendly, aspirational atmosphere for your students. Whenever you think about implementing restorative practices, you should ask yourself: "What is it that you are restoring?" This will give you a better idea of what practices to implement, and how to approach your team when introducing these practices. Because we have a house system that makes students feel like they belong, we are typically restoring our school from the harm that took place in that positive environment. When it comes to this aspect of restoration, there are many things you can do to achieve the same end-goal. Here are some more examples for you:

- **Get to know each of your students by name**

    As a leader, how can you restore your community when you don't even know your students' names? As the leader of your school (or one of the leaders), you should make it a point to learn the names of all your students. This makes you more personable, more approachable, and more genuine. Therefore, you should challenge yourself to get to know all of your students. Each time the school year starts, take the time to politely ask the name of each student. To make it easier for you to remember their names, ask them a couple of questions to get to know them better too.

    Personally, I have thought of a fun way to learn the names of the students in my school, called the "Name Pie Challenge." For this, I give myself a deadline—usually between 45 and 60 days—to learn all the names of my students. Setting this deadline gives me a stronger sense of accountability, which also motivates me. I learn my students' names by attending their classes and participating in their community-building circles. Whenever I get the chance, I study their ID photos, I stand in front of the school each morning to greet them, and I say their names out loud every time I see them.

Then comes the fun part. At the end of my self-imposed deadline, I go around the school and allow the students whose names I don't know to pie me in the face! Of course, since I really don't like whipped cream, I make sure that I have memorized all of my students' names so I don't have to get pied in the face. Fortunately, things will get easier the more that you practice. As time goes by, you will eventually learn all the names of your students (to date, the most I have been pied in the face has been four times).

- **Build an aggressively friendly atmosphere**

As much as possible, be overly friendly. As the leader, you should be so friendly that you are asked to stop being friendly. Try to mingle with everyone in your school. This is the first step in building a friendlier atmosphere. After all, your students won't see you as friendly or approachable if you're always cooped up in your office. Greet everyone you meet, and when someone greets you first, always greet them back. These simple steps will already increase the warmth of your school's atmosphere.

- **Own transitions and lunch time**

Transition time is a great time to build relationships with students and revolutionize your school's culture. During these times, you can play music, and have fun activities like having secret handshakes and learning your students' names as they walk to their destination. Lunchtime is a great time to make the atmosphere more fun, too. During lunch, I always make an effort to go into all areas of the campus to sit and meet with students so that I can learn more about them. On many days, I bring out the speakers and become "DJ Principal Rahh" for my students. These are some fun ways to build a revolutionary school culture.

- **Language matters**

Whenever you are communicating with others, try to use inclusive language for all genders, sexual orientations, and races. This will break down the walls between yourself and the people around you. Language matters a lot. One simple, yet impactful, way to make things more inclusive is by changing the names of regular gatherings like assemblies and advisories to words like 'Kinship' and 'Family'. At my school, we changed the name of one of the standard advisory classes by calling it 'kinship'. This change helped shift the language, as well as the action used in the class toward connection.

We also started calling our assemblies 'family', since these assemblies give us the opportunity to all come together, much like a family. The beauty behind Family is that we start with it each Monday. Family in our school is a 35-minute gathering wherein we inspire our students to try to be better than their best every day. Typically, Family involves a speech given by myself or a guest, plus an activity to inspire greatness. Now, our students know that every Monday, Family takes place, and it has become a kind of sacred tradition that we all look forward to. Do you have traditions like this in your school?

This is just one example of how using the right language can spur amazing change. It's also a good idea to include diverse literature in your school's library and in the classrooms, to help your students learn and appreciate diversity more. In line with this, you should also use character education words like honesty, acceptance, and respect as part of your language. We adopted books such as *The Hate U Give* by Angie Thomas, and *Dear Martin* by Nic Stone as school-wide literature for students to have discourse around.

## Building a Culture That Lasts

The culture that you create will help you prosper far beyond your expectations. Through the years, such a culture increases your school's reputation, while ensuring that everyone who steps inside your structure feels happy and safe. Create a system that will continue being efficient even after you, your staff, and your teachers will leave your school in the future. Here are some ways for you to do this:

### *Build a Clock*

I once went to a workshop in Chicago where a presenter said that when building a school culture, the goal should be to build a clock. At that time, I really didn't understand what he meant. He further explained how this is a very clever phrase with a deep meaning for school culture. Simply put, if you realize that people keep asking you what time it is, build a clock for them. In your school, if you find your teachers and staff asking you about every little thing—and they will when you start making all of these changes—things might become too tiring or even frustrating to continually answer similar questions.

To avoid this, and to empower your people, create a symbolic clock. A guide that will propel your school to greatness. Instead of becoming your school's "time-teller," you become its clock-builder. The clock you will build comes in the form of your school's standard operating procedures (SOPs). Here are some steps to help you build this:

- Go through your school's existing SOPs to determine which ones you need to keep, remove, and change.

- Brainstorm new SOPs to ensure that your school's new culture continues even if you are no longer at the school. Invite your teachers and staff to help you brainstorm. This is the best way to empower them.

- As a team, implement all of your SOPs, both old and new. These hands-on practices will make you see what works and what doesn't. Implementing the SOPs together also transforms your team into time-tellers and clock-builders just like you.

## *Step Back and Observe*

After giving your teachers and staff the power to continue working to maintain the culture you all collectively have built, take a step back to observe. Observe your teachers, the members of your staff, and how well they implement the processes and procedures that have been created together. Whenever you have a new teacher or staff member, allow them to introduce the SOPs. Also, observe how well your team guides the students. At the end of the day, you will know that you have created a culture that will last long if it endures even if you step back and take yourself out of the equation. I can tell you that there is not a dollar amount that can equal the value of the feeling when you witness the manifestation of a vision. When you can achieve this, you can move on to the next principle in the process of starting an educational revolution...

## Take Time to Reflect

No matter how bad your school's culture is right now, you can always do things to make it better. Even if you think that you have a culture that is already ideal for your students, you may want to take a second look at it. Remember that the best school culture is one that accepts all students and provides opportunities for everyone to grow, not just the most privileged ones. As you evaluate this aspect of your school, try to be as honest as possible. Now that you have reached the end of this chapter, it's time to reflect and answer the following questions:

- How can you and your other school leaders support your teachers and staff in adopting new practices?

- What models of instruction will enable your classrooms to be more responsive to a full range of learners?

- Are questions, creativity, originality, and new ideas welcome in your school?

Is your school a safe place to take academic, creative, or revolutionary risks?

Chapter 9:

# Principle 4: Revolutionizing Your School Culture using Social Media and Technology

*"In education, technology can be a life-changer, a game-changer, for kids who are both in school and out of school."* (Queen Rania)

Yes, even queens see the importance of using technology and modern methods to improve different aspects of education. In recent years, technology has made such a huge impact on all parts of our lives. Communication via social media platforms, in particular, has become very easy and convenient. Concurrently, learning has become richer, thanks to online methods and resources. As a revolutionary educator, you should take advantage of technology, as it can help put your school on the map. In this chapter, you will learn how to leverage technology and social media for your school's branding. By doing this, you can increase the positivity of your school culture, while creating a virtual village.

## The Importance of Establishing an Online Presence

Right now, social media has become such a huge part of our lives that the younger generation might not understand how life used to be without it! Social media is here to stay, and you can use this to your advantage by establishing an online presence. I believe every seasoned educator above the age of 35 should have a mentor who is under the age of 25. Trust me, you will thank me later. As you work to improve your school, you can stay hungry by entering the online world with a mentor who understands it better than you. Here are some important reasons why you should seriously have a social media presence:

- **To share information easily**

  By creating accounts for your school on different social media platforms, you can share information with parents and students, both existing and prospective. You can even share photos, videos, and posts on your page to share valuable information with your community. These days, sharing is one of the most popular methods of communication, and if you keep your school's social media accounts active, this will generate a lot of interest. This can go a long way, especially if you want to encourage parents to enroll their children at your school.

- **To provide updates**

  Another benefit of establishing an online presence is to make it easier for you to share news, updates, and important information to your students, parents, teachers, and staff members. You can even share links for downloadable newsletters. In particular, your students and parents will appreciate this a lot. Through social media, you can keep everyone abreast of the latest events and news in your school. All I ask is that you make it unique.

- **To promote your school**

  Promoting your school is very easy through social media platforms and other online methods. You should never stop promoting your school. If your school has a website, you can add the link to your social media accounts to make it easier for people to find your site. Another great tip is to link and sync all of your online accounts and platforms. That way, people who are interested in learning more about your school won't have any difficulty finding what they need.

- **To strengthen the identity of your school**

  This benefit is related to the previous one. As you promote your school online, you can share information about it. Doing this allows people, especially those who aren't affiliated with your school, to see what kind of culture you have. Your culture is queen and king of your school so promote it. All these efforts you put into sharing and promoting will strengthen your school's identity, especially within your community.

- **To engage with your community**

  Through social media and other online platforms, you can communicate with the members of your community, not just those who work in or go to your school. You can establish professional and social relationships, which could turn into strong links over time. As the leader of a school, this is a very important benefit, especially if you want to reach out to significant members of your community and create lasting relationships.

- **It's free!**

  The best part about establishing an online presence and using it to your advantage is that it's totally free. That is, unless you want to pay for advertisements. Usually, though, you don't have to use paid advertisements for this. Just keeping your accounts active and replying to everyone who communicates with you about your school is enough.

## Creating Your School Brand

Now that you understand how valuable social media and online platforms are, the next thing to do is to start creating your online presence. While this might seem complex or overwhelming, you can have a lot of fun with this process. Personally, I had to learn many things to get the word out there, but I did get a lot of valuable help and insight from my team.

If you're not tech-savvy, you really need to have a mentor. But if you don't have one, you can always ask for help from your teachers, staff members, and even your students. Then, you can establish your online presence in the following ways:

## Create a Website for Your School

There's nothing more impressive than a school with a well-made interactive website. Your brand must reflect excellence throughout all platforms. When prospective parents and students want to learn more about your school, they can do so through your website. And if you can add links on your site to your social media accounts, people who visit your site will have a more fulfilling interactive experience. Creating such a website requires a lot of skill and technical experience. If none of you have the skills to do this, then you can outsource the work. The main thing is that your brand stays consistent and that the experience for the user is top-notch.

## Create a Facebook Profile

Facebook is one of the most popular social media platforms now. By creating a Facebook profile for your school, you can update people with stories of achievement and interest in your school. You can also sell your school's merchandise on there as well. You can share news, photos, videos, and other valuable content for everyone to share, remember your school's story can land you additional resources and partnerships. Now that you have chosen to start an educational revolution on Facebook, remember this kind of momentum can be used to create a movement that can be highly aspirational for your school community. And the more you can share, the more you can inspire others to join your school.

## Explore Different Social Media Platforms

Of course, Facebook isn't the only social media platform you can take advantage of. There are many others, such as Instagram, Twitter, and TikTok. Ask your teachers and staff if any of them have experience with social media marketing. Having a team member with such experience will be extremely helpful, as you can come up with a plan for which platforms to use and how to use them effectively. Our school is on multiple platforms that are all meant to serve a different purpose. Knowing your audience is essential as you grow your brand.

## Social Media Management

Social media isn't something that you start and then leave. You have to continuously manage your online profiles to ensure that your presence endures. You can either assign someone to take charge of each social media profile your school has, or you can do it yourself by setting a time for this each day. I typically set my content to automatically post on a predetermined day and time to assist me with managing. When it comes to social media management, learning how to strategize is key.

## The Power of Social Media

Social media has the power that you can use to transform the trajectory of your classrooms, school, district, and community.

When I opened my school, I had a vision of all kinds of transformations, but I didn't have enough social capital to do these things. Of course, I didn't give up. Instead, I began to hawk influencers by sending them DMs, asking them if they would like to visit my school to speak with my students. As I went through this long process, I came across a rap artist by the name of Stix. He is a Watts, California native, and an activist for Watts. When I sent him a DM asking him to visit my school, he gladly agreed.

When Stix visited our school, he was amazed by everything that was going on—and wanted to add value to it. He leveraged his relationships with the Los Angeles Clippers and LAFC Pro Soccer team to provide our school with a new gymnasium, outdoor courts, and even an urban garden. Shortly after Planet Fitness heard about the movement, the company offered to rebuild our entire weight room while offering health and wealth management, free of charge. After that, the Banc of California offered to provide resources for Financial Literacy instruction. They even provided a free program for our students. Our school gained all of these just because I sent a direct message via Instagram.

And this is the true power of social media.

Social media has changed our lives so much that we cannot help but take notice. As a school leader, it is your responsibility to learn everything you can about social media and how to utilize it for the benefit of your school. As I have shared, one of the most important impacts of social media is to help you get resources for your school. But before you introduce yourself to significant people through social media, make sure that your school has something amazing, powerful, or unique to offer. This will help you grab the attention of those to whom you are sending messages. Fortunately, you are already reading this book, which means that you are about to embark on a journey to make your school stand out from the rest.

Aside from helping your school grow, social media also has the power to build a more positive community within the school itself. You can use social media to promote your school's branding along with the marketing of your school's mission, vision, mantra, and core values.

# The Keys to Leveraging Social Media to Obtain Sponsors and Partners

If you want people to take enough interest in your school to help you grow and improve it, you need to learn the art of leveraging social media. This is another way you can revolutionize your classroom or school culture. For this, you may want to take inspiration from Alfred Shivy Brooks, better known by his Instagram handle, @callmeshivy.

Alfred leveraged his social media account to live-stream his Government and Economics class in Atlanta. That way, his students who couldn't attend his class physically could still join virtually. When he saw how successful this method was, Alfred took it up a notch by spreading the love around his campus. Alfred started a movement called "Teacher Talk Tuesday," in which he went around campus asking his staff and students to finish culturally relevant sentences. After gathering their responses, he posted these on his page.

The movement allowed him to build relationships with partners like Papa John's (yes, the pizza place), which then allowed him to conduct a "Feed the Kids" campaign, wherein he, Papa John's, and educators across the nation fed kids in the middle of the COVID pandemic. Now, Alfred hosts a weekly show on his Instagram page called "Teacher Talk Live," in which he provides a voice for his students, while leveraging his social capital to empower his students. Comedians, artists, and athletes have all come to speak with his class. Remarkably, he even hosted a virtual prom for his students—all because he learned how to leverage social media.

Interesting, isn't it? But how do you do this? Here are some key steps for you to follow:

- **Create a school-wide tagline or hashtag**

   Whenever you will post something on any of your social media accounts, use the tagline or hashtag you create. That way, when people click on it or try to search for it, they will gain access to almost everything you have posted. For this, try to think of something catchy, creative, relatable, and easy to remember–something that will stick in the mind of anyone who reads it. The hashtag is like your digital portfolio of content.

- **Create your school's ethical bribe**

An ethical bribe is a free resource that you would use as bait. The purpose of an ethical bribe is to get permission to access a person's contact details so that you can reach out to them in the future. Generally, the only details you will get through an ethical bribe are a person's name and email address. When choosing an ethical bribe, it must be attractive, unique, related to your content, and utterly irresistible. It should also provide value to your target audience. Also, you should use ethical bribes responsibly so that you don't end up causing more harm than good. We used an ethical bribe on our Instagram page around attendance. We wanted more students to engage with our page so we created a post and explained to students that if they would like, share, and tag two of their friends on the post that they will enter a chance to win a free dress pass, or item from or student store. It was a successful post and it got more students to engage and follow the page.

- **Offer fun promotions**

Whenever you host something online like meetings or video conferences, offer promotions like freebies to all students, parents, or guardians who will like or follow your page. You can also offer promotions at strategic times, like right before enrollment and during the summer, for example. These will hook your audiences and make them more interested in what you have to offer.

- **Create a campaign to engage your audience**

  This is an excellent way to generate interest and gather followers. The campaigns you create can be about an event at your school, an important cause, or something relevant to your school's mission and vision. To create the campaign, you must:

  - Know what goal you are striving to achieve.

  - Decide which social media platform on which to launch your campaign.

  - Create different types of content for your campaign.

  - Create a schedule for when you will post your content.

  - Keep track of the people joining your campaign and interact with them. If necessary, follow up after your campaign has finished.

- **Update, update, update!**

  Finally, make sure that your social media accounts are always updated. They should show your school in real life. The key here is to show the world that your school is filled with love, respect, and acceptance—which makes it easy for you to capture genuine moments in time. Document your school's activities and events, and then showcase these on your page. This will help increase engagement.

## Maximizing the Effectiveness of Your Online Presence

After you have created all of your school's social media accounts and profiles, it's time to start optimizing them. Remember: social media isn't just about creating something and leaving it alone. Your online presence needs a lot of TLC, especially if you want to maximize its impact. For all of your online platforms, remember that small details matter. People online tend to be very critical, so you don't want to give them a reason to find something wrong with your school. Also, remember that the experience you provide to your students and parents on your social media platforms will be compared with other schools, and even other businesses. This is why it's important to plan these things out and to use them properly. Here are some tips on how to do this:

- **TikTok**

  Have you ever watched those countless TikTok videos that are all over the Internet? If you're on social media, chances are, you have already encountered such videos. You can sign up on TikTok and use this as a platform to reach out to and engage with your students. Building community through Tiktok is a great way to maximize your presence. By sharing videos on this wildly popular app, you can build a fun virtual village.

- **Instagram**

  Instagram is another popular social media platform where you can share photos to communicate, express, and reach out to students, parents, and even members of your community. By putting your school on Instagram, you can even inspire influencers to take notice. When this happens, your school's image gets an instant boost, which might even propel you to greatness!

There are so many other platforms out there to use. For instance, if you want to share educational videos, you can post these on YouTube. Or if you want to create regular articles about school-related topics, you can do so through a blog. The point here is that you can maximize social media by using the platforms in the best possible way.

## Take Time to Reflect

During the writing of this book, our world is currently at the mercy of COVID-19, which has become a global pandemic. Because of this, online learning and social media have become even more important. Schools all over the world have turned to technology to continue reaching out to students by building a virtual community. This means that now is the best time to start learning how to use technology and social media to your advantage. Now that you have learned the basics of how to do this, it's time to answer the following questions as you reflect on what you have learned:

- Right now, how are you using social media to increase and promote your school culture?

- What messages do you want to get across to your target audience?

- Who will benefit from the information you want to convey?

- How will they benefit from what you have to offer?

Chapter 10:

# Principle 5: Revolutionizing Your Data-Centered Culture

*"Data are just summaries of thousands of stories—tell a few of those stories to help make the data meaningful."* (Heath)

In line with the previous chapter, you should also try to revolutionize your school's culture by making it more data centered. Technology and social media will help you spread the word about your school, but you shouldn't stop there. You should take things further by creating a system to gather data for you to analyze and make even more improvements in the future. This is one of the more technical aspects of your revolutionary journey, but it can also be very interesting—and a lot of fun! It's all about diving into the process with the right perspective to find out what really matters when it comes to students.

## Measuring What Matters for Student Success

*"When an organization isn't ready for total openness, culture work may be needed before data could be centered and implemented."* (Cole).

As you work to change your school for the better, you should still focus on the most important part of your school: your students. There would be no point in making things better if your students are struggling with their studies. To help you and the rest of your team understand your students better, you need to think of ways to measure what matters for student success. This will help you determine the steps or interventions to help your students succeed in your school and in the future. The things to measure are:

- **Focus on competency and mastery rather than ranking students.**

  The things that happen in the classroom are the main things that affect students' learning. You can only measure this by creating a criterion for student success. In order to complete this, I encourage you to reflect on your academic philosophy and your grading philosophy. This is the time you reflect deeply on your mission as an educator. Once you answer these questions it should guide you on what you should measure in your classroom and school.

- **Essential factors**

  Although academic performance is important, non-cognitive essential factors are vital to student success too. These include confidence, motivation, and resiliency. You can measure these through written assessments or in-person interviews with the students. These can be done by classroom teachers or school-wide intentional levers.

- **Level of engagement with extracurricular activities**

  This shows how connected students feel with any activities that they take part in outside of your classroom. Such activities are also important, as they help students unwind, get to know each other better, and have fun. If you notice any students who aren't engaged with these activities, you may need to see what additional activities can be implemented to engage them.

- **Usage of campus resources**

  This refers to how your students use the resources available in your school, if they make the most of your school's facilities, and if these resources are making a difference in your students' learning. You must consistently check the equity, effectiveness and efficiency of all resources on your campus. You can keep track of this usage through check-in apps, meeting debriefs, data-trackers or logbooks. Then you can determine how these resources are helping your students based on their performances in class.

- **Creating creative and practical predictors**

Analytical predictors have been proven to not be in the best interest of students. Therefore, you can recreate predictors of multiple forms of brilliance so you can obtain multiple scores through assessments. This is very important to help you pinpoint any students who need more love and attention. These scores can also give you a better understanding of the things you can do to improve students' performances in the different areas and lead them to success.

- **Adult interactions**

Through the course of a term or a semester, students will engage with teachers, staff members, and even you, as the principal. As these interactions happen, you should all increase your awareness as students might reveal information that can indicate struggles or difficulties. By catching these indications, you can find the best way to support your students that need more love. For instance, in my school, the goal I have is for my students to feel connected to at least three adults on our campus.

- **Responses to assessments**

Finally, you should have regular assessments, both cognitive and non-cognitive to determine how your students are doing in their classes. Cognitive assessments come in the form of quizzes and tests, while non-cognitive ones come in the form of surveys. These assessments will provide you with the insight you need to promote student achievement.

## Strategies for Building a Data-Driven Culture

To build a data-driven culture, you must learn how to focus on data-driven facts rooted in what matters for achieving your mission. In this world, a data-driven culture is important, as you can use it to leverage insights in each department in your school. At our school, we leverage data through our departments and our house system, making it connect with all the students and educators. The main goal of building such a culture is to utilize data actively to help your school improve the magic that happens daily in the classroom and the hallways. This allows you to utilize your school's potential to the highest level as the decisions you make turn out to be more successful and effective. It will also help you connect your school's mission, vision, mantra, and core values with the data you gather to improve the outcomes for young people. You can build your own data-driven culture in your school by implementing these strategies:

- **Implement a Data Cycle**

  Does your school have a data cycle? Before you can make any change in your current culture, you should first encourage your team to make these changes with you. Introduce the concept of a data-analysis cycle to them and help them understand its importance. We implement a data analysis protocol every month to determine our current position and next steps.

- **Clean-up your data**

  Next, take a look at the current data your school has. Ask yourself, "Does this data matter? Does it connect to our vision and mission?" Before you start changing this, you should take steps to improve the quality and structure of your data by using the right methods and tools. You can also ask experts for advice on how you can do this.

- **Choose your metrics carefully**

When it comes to data collection, metrics refer to the methods you plan to use to measure progress or performance. In the previous section, I shared with you a number of metrics for you to focus on to help you understand your students better. Now, it's time to choose which of those metrics to use, and to even add more if you think it's necessary.

- **Improve your data literacy**

If you don't want to struggle in your data-driven culture, you must take the necessary steps to improve your data literacy, or how you understand the data you will gather. This improvement helps you make better and smarter data-based decisions. If needed, provide your team with the opportunity for specialized training. This is essential, especially if most of your teachers and staff (even yourself) feel intimidated at the mere thought of gathering, interpreting, and analyzing data.

- **Make your data transparent**

Make your data transparent with your staff. You might have some staff members feel uncomfortable, but it is necessary to get to the desired state for your school. Making your data transparent is an excellent way to make it easier for yourself and your whole team to analyze data and make decisions. If your staff is resistant, leverage the "QTIP Strategy," which means to **Q**uit **T**aking **I**t **P**ersonally. With the help of QTIP, you can come up with a way to make data-informed decisions.

- **Take ownership of the data and don't be afraid to be vulnerable**

   As the leader, this is your data. Own it. Speak about your flaws and weaknesses, and how you may have impacted the data. For many people, this kind of change is huge. Therefore, some of your team members might find value in how you deal with reflecting on the data, especially if the data is currently not the best. If you can help your team understand this process better, overcome their uncertainty, and have ownership over their data too, it will become easier to work together to achieve a more data-centered culture.

   With all the things you need to do as part of this change, the final tip I have for you is to always stay connected to what really matters. These concepts and processes are quite challenging to implement, but you are up for it. After you are done with the next section, you might wonder how you managed things before you entered your data-driven culture!

## Tips for Collecting Data

Before you can start using relevant data to learn more about your students, teachers, staff, and school, you must first learn how to collect data correctly. Data collection is essential, especially if you want to collect data that you can use. I, myself, have always collected data every two weeks as benchmarks, once a month to determine success, and every three months to determine adjustments. To accomplish this, you have to have an established data collection protocol. Here are some of the most effective tips that I have learned through experience:

- When you choose a data collection method, use it consistently. You may have to learn about different methods and try each one out before you find one that suits your school perfectly.

- Make sure that the data collection method you use is sustainable. When you find "the one," stick with it. For example, we use a method called, '#TurninTuesday'. Turn in Tuesday is a bi-weekly reminder for teachers to submit data in regards to their primary metric.

- Accountability of Praise for your digital data. Praise your students and staff for meeting the metrics. We have what is called, '#WinItWednesday'. Win it Wednesday is a bi-weekly or once a month celebration for classrooms and teachers who met or exceeded the metrics.

- If you plan to collect data to analyze, make sure that the data you collect is representative. This will give you more accurate results. You can collect data on essential groups such as English learners, exceptional needs, African American male and female students, etc.

Data collection is an essential part of your data-driven culture. Fortunately, it's one of the easiest aspects for you to learn. Once you get the hang of it, you can start using the data you have gathered.

## How to Use School Data

After you have collected all of the data you need, you can start using it for various purposes. You can use school data to understand things better, make smarter decisions, and even create plans for your revolutionary changes. How data will be used depends on the person who will use it. Since we are focused on an educational setting, let's take a look at the different ways you can use the data you collect:

## *Using Data as a School Leader*

As a school leader, you can use data in the following ways:

- To compare different departments or classes for the purpose of finding out what works and what doesn't.

- To not only inform your teachers about how they can improve their classroom practices, but also reflect on how you can improve your leadership practices.

- To use as a guide for when you are planning activities for professional development.

- To help you create and organize school-wide programs for learning support.

- To screen students and identify those who are eligible for specialized programs.

- To provide your students with useful feedback.

- To inform the parents of your students about their performance in school, both academic and non-academic.

- To provide accurate and valuable reports to your community.

## Using Data as a Teacher

As for your teachers, you can teach them to use data in the following ways:

- To use as evidence of the skills and knowledge that the students have learned.

- To use for assessing experimental teaching practices.

- To make comparisons against cohorts.

- To come up with ways to collaborate with other teachers.

- To use as a guide for assessments against your school's expected learning standards and outcomes.

- To use as a reference when reporting to parents about student performance.

With all of these in mind, you can now make a decision as to what type of data you need to gather.

## Take Time to Reflect

Creating a data-centered culture doesn't have to be a challenge. As with the other steps you need to take, learning what you can and applying what you learn will help you out immensely. Add practice to the mix and you will surely succeed in creating this kind of culture in your school. Now that this chapter has ended, it's time to answer the following questions as part of your self-reflection:

- What data should you collect?

- Why should you collect such data?

- What methods should you use in collecting the data you need?

- Who should be involved in the process of data collection?

# Chapter 11:

# Principle 6: Revolutionizing Teaching and Learning

*"If your actions inspire others to dream more, learn more, do more and become more, you are a leader."* (Adams)

There is nothing better than the "aha moment" that takes place when students master content. As an educator, teaching and learning are the focal points of your leadership role. As a teacher, I always approached my classroom by reflecting on my philosophy, and that started with my grading practices. I always felt that the traditional grading system was a reinforcement of classism. A's were equivalent to the "ruling class", B's to the "high class", C's to the 'middle class", D's to the "low class", and F's to the "poverty class". Therefore, my thought process was that I refused to build upon what I call the pipeline to poverty. In addition to this ideology, I accompany that with the fact that racism is a tool to reinforce classism, so the intersectionality of both always made me approach my teaching and learning with a mastery concept. I might add that because I felt the system was rigged to keep students of color suppressed and oppressed, let's just say my grading practices as a teacher came in the form of reparations. I don't mean that I gave students handouts, however, it meant the opposite—it meant that I asked myself 'what did the actual letter grade really mean? I knew students were forced to be eligible for college but my mission was to get them ready for life. I could not neglect that students of color need to know their truth so I tasked myself to fill the minds of my students with sacred knowledge because, as Marcus Garvey once said, "A people without knowledge of their past history, origin, and culture is like a tree without roots." Therefore, the system has failed our children... So why would I?

To revolutionize the educational experience, you must inspire and empower your teachers. That way, they can effectively teach our future leaders of tomorrow. You must also challenge the current frames of thought and mindsets about growth and success. In this chapter, we will go through the revolutionary methods of improving teaching and learning processes. After learning different techniques and strategies from the chapters you have read thus far, ask yourself: Why is teaching and learning this far down? As per experience, I have seen that most leaders focus more on micromanaging teachers to make sure that they turn in great lesson plans instead of creating an amazing environment in which teachers can conduct great lessons. This is something you should dwell on as you go through this chapter. Although we are almost at the end of your learning journey, there is still much to learn.

## Culturally Responsive Teaching

*"A teacher that refuses to see culture or race, is like an artist that doesn't see the beauty in the colour palette."* (Rahh)

For many years, schools have fought against having discussions around culture, race, and diversity in the classroom. A challenge for many schools is to understand, recognize and respond to the cultural differences and needs of students. Like the above mentioned quote it is important for educators to see and acknowledge the beauty in their students' culture. I was having a discussion with a group of educators and was asked "Could a teacher that neglects to see race and culture be culturally responsive?" The question triggered rich discourse around how to implement culturally responsive pedagogy. As a school leader it will be critical for you to facilitate a safe space around race and culture in your school. Becoming a culturally responsive school isn't extra work, it's the actual work.

## *Culturally Responsive Environment*

Build in the following ways:

- *It begins with the environment.* Your school or classroom should be focused on everyone feeling like they have a voice and belong. (never stop building community)

- *Start with a conversation.* Facilitate meetings around thought questions around students' cultural identity. (Is it important for students to know their history?)

- *Build upon the conversation.* Have deeper conversations around the staff's cultural and sub-cultural differences. (What are the values?)

- *Form a collective vision and mission around identity and culture.* What are the outcomes? (Our students will achieve excellence by knowing themselves in context to the world.)

- *Value self and cultural discovery.* Use student autonomy as a guide for lessons and measuring against your school's outcomes.

- *Consult with experts and the community.* Be inclusive, bring in experts to learn from and grow your knowledge.

This journey is not a destination, it is a constant ever evolving mechanism that should be fluid within your classroom and school. The key will be to build an environment that welcomes tough conversations. I recommend having a strong culture around discourse before jumping into this headfirst. I have personally witnessed it become extremely difficult for leaders when jumping into this work without having a positive environment. To engineer these types of meetings, it will be critical for you to be the lead learner and facilitator. This is a unique skillset that has to be developed to push the work ahead.

## Humane-Oriented Teaching

Through my experience, I have found that leaders who have created an environment and culture of learning had a much easier time increasing the level of rigor in the classroom by being a Humanistic Leader.

Humanist education began early in the 1900s, when humanists thought that the main educational theories—psychoanalysis and behaviorism— were not ideal, as their perception of learners was too negative. Instead of supporting and encouraging learners, these theories focused on "fixing" them. Since humanists didn't agree with this perception and the methods used in both theories, they developed humanistic education. This revolutionary theory allowed educators to focus on helping learners bring out their best selves.

Therefore, as a humane-oriented leader, you must inspire your teachers to encourage their students to act and think critically, hand-in-hand with the values of humanity. By taking the humanist approach, your teachers will focus on the emotional wellbeing of their students by seeing them as innately good at their very core. This approach is based on the following philosophical pillars:

- **Emotions affect learning,** so you need to help students achieve a positive emotional state to help them perform well and strive to be the best versions of themselves.

- **Free will** can be given by allowing your students to make their own choice in terms of pathways for assignment completion and work.

- **Innate goodness** means that you should see all people as innately good (presume positive intentions).

- **Intrinsic motivation** means that we all have an innate desire to become the best versions of ourselves, so you should encourage this as an educator.

Every classroom should have this as a standard so while you and your teachers are creating this movement with students and investing in the humanistic approach, you as the leader must also treat your teachers the same way. That is the only way this can realistically work. As a school leader, one of the most effective ways of teaching this approach is by showing them how it's done. Within the humanistic education approach, you will try to awaken another person's need to be the best version of themselves by helping them develop intrinsic motivation.

This approach isn't very common in schools, which is why you may have to rethink your perception of education. When you think about it, this approach will make teaching and learning a lot easier. If your teachers can successfully awaken their students' intrinsic motivation, they will always stay hungry no matter what challenges come their way. To start taking the humanistic approach, here are some strategies:

- Teachers must be a role model for all the habits, attitudes, and beliefs that you wish to foster. This is why you must first get investment from your teachers before they can start practicing these strategies with their students.

- Create mission statements every year as these relate to their students' learning journey. Teachers should create personal goals for their class every year. Make sure that these goals are both challenging and realistic. That way, your students will feel highly motivated to achieve them.

- Give your students the opportunity to choose their own mission and goal for the year. Provide them with a selection of tasks and activities to choose from, all of which will help them learn the concepts they need.

- Plan to have plenty of group activities for your students to participate in. Cooperative learning is essential, as it helps develop your students' affective and social skills.

- Empower self-discovery and exploration in the classroom. As facilitators we help move the discussions along, while allowing the students to talk among themselves to explore.

Have you ever thought about your own skills as an educator? If you are like me, you started out as a teacher and moved your way up to becoming a school leader. But sometimes, school leaders forget how it feels to be a teacher. Sadly, I have seen that some school principals are overly critical of their teachers, while knowing that they, themselves, were not the best teachers. Let's face it, some educators unfortunately strive to become school leaders to get further away from children.

Don't let your position dictate the way you relate to your teachers. If you were trained by an overly critical or strict principal, try to remember what it felt like back then. As a humanistic leader, you want to encourage your teachers and make them feel good about themselves. When they feel this way, their confidence will start increasing, along with their attitude towards you, your school, and the students. Trust me it will impact the classroom environment.

## Redefining the Role of a Teacher

*"When you control a man's thinking you do not have to worry about his actions. You do not have to tell him not to stand here or go yonder. He will find his 'proper place' and will stay in it. You do not need to send him to the back door. He will go without being told. In fact, if there is no back door, he will cut one for his special benefit. His education makes it necessary."* (Woodson).

The quote above is very powerful. How do you, your staff, your teachers, and your school dismantle the white supremacy that exists inside of your world as educators?

Do you know what your role is, as a teacher? Before I explain this part, let me share a story with you.

As a student, my intelligence was always questioned by teachers because of the way I walked, dressed, delivered messages or how I expressed my thoughts. I am sure you have students that can relate. Although, a student's brilliance shouldn't just be tied to their English, writing, and math scores. While these analytical measures are important, they impact and influence the practice of educators to continue analytical teaching strategies that neglect the creative and practical intelligence of students.

Robert J. Sternberg, the famous psychologist, sees intelligence, not as a narrow, monolithic quality that makes you good at chess or get good grades. Instead, it is an interplay between the practical, creative, and analytical aspects of your mind. Sternberg calls this the "Triarchic Theory of Intelligence":

- **Practical intelligence** involves your ability to handle daily tasks in the real world. Some call this "street smarts" because they show how you relate to your external environment.

- **Creative intelligence** involves thinking creatively and adjusting effectively to new situations.

- **Analytical intelligence** involves your pure brainpower that you use to process information.

Personally, my call-to-action is that we should value our practical and creative intelligence just as much as we value our analytical intelligence. My reason for this is that we have been attempting to solve creative problems in our society for years with 'analytical' solutions. But inequity, race relations, and marginalized practices aren't skills that are just developed. At my school, our mission is for every student to achieve self-actualization—one of our basic needs. We conduct "presentations of learning," which are a kind of rite of passage that each student performs to move on to the next grade. These presentations of learning have a composite score, in which we rigorously train our teachers, industry professionals, and community volunteers to review and implement as panelists for each student.

As you can see, a teacher's role isn't as simple as it might seem. Although our existing educational system isn't ideal, I do see some amazing changes happening. Prompted by massive revolutions in information technology, knowledge, and public demand for better learning, schools all over the country are slowly but surely restructuring themselves. Just like in my own school, revolutions are happening, and it's time for you to join us.

As Revolutionary educators, you and your teachers shouldn't just focus on caring for students, dispensing information, and sorting them according to their academic skills. Instead, you should start adapting new practices that will acknowledge the science and art of learning, not just one or the other. Essentially, your role as an educator or a teacher is to be caring and knowledgeable so that you can make your students feel secure and motivated to find their purpose.

Another important role you hold as an educator is to individualize your students. Rather than thinking of your students as one whole class, you should focus on each of them individually. Do this so that you can understand their unique cultural and social backgrounds, interests, abilities, learning styles, and needs. In order to fully do this, you have to ask a couple of questions. Like I mentioned previously you must ask yourself, how is your school planning your lessons to be culturally aware? Second, how are you implementing the lessons to be culturally responsive? Third, how are your students being impacted to determine if you are culturally competent? The goal is cultural competence in every piece of content and in every class. In your class, do your students see themselves as they are, feel like themselves, and believe in themselves? It's time to learn how to become better educators by changing the way you see teaching. As your school family goes on a revolutionary journey learning to do all these things, it will provide your students with the opportunity to find their hidden treasure.

Finally, you can also try to build what I call "protective knowledge", which is the ability to teach students how to be guards at the gates of their minds. Only substance may enter. This simply means that you and your teachers should help your students learn how to be cautious about the information they consume and believe. That way, you don't have to worry about them believing the "fake news" when they are in different environments.

## Take Time to Reflect

As simple as this chapter may have been, it was short and sweet enough to impart valuable information to you as a school leader. Even though people look up to you as a leader, you should still see yourself as a teacher, of both students and teachers alike. Before moving on to the last principle of your revolutionary education journey, think about the answers to these questions:

- Do you have any existing practices that fit into the humanistic approach?

- What is the main role of your grading practices?

- Why are you failing students if you believe the system has failed the students?

Since teachers are the "heartbeat of your school," what should you do to help inspire them?

# Chapter 12:

# Revolutionizing Your Community

*"Revolution is a serious thing, the most serious thing about a revolutionary's life. When one commits oneself to the struggle, it must be for a lifetime."* (Davis).

In this final chapter, we will be focusing on the community to which your school belongs. To increase the likelihood of succeeding in your revolutionary journey, you must go beyond your school and reach out to your community. In this chapter, you will be learning some tips and strategies to create your own five-year plan to make your school community a prosperous and empowered one. By involving the community in your school, you will gain added support, not just financially, but also in hands-on participation for the success of your school and students.

## Creating an Ecosystem for Your School Community

As a Revolutionary Principal, another call-to-action I have is to truly create a school ecosystem that tackles five important things:

- **Education**

  This is what we should be doing right as a school. Prepare your students for "college and career" so that you can prepare them for life! Education has to be rooted in sacred knowledge for students to be fully equipped to deal with the challenges of today's world. That 'straight A', gifted student, without the lessons and values of sacred knowledge is like an expensive luxury car with no gas. It is literally useless without the fuel to drive it. Therefore, the need for *Sankofa*-like principles and sacred knowledge is a must for all schools.

- ## Economics

Financial literacy and macroeconomics are very important in black and brown communities. Black and brown spending power is much different than black and brown economic power. Structurally, our public schools aren't teaching financial literacy at the level it needs to be taught. I don't think it is by accident either. In order for the community to flourish, the cycle of the dollar must increase. In order for this cycle to increase, the future generation must understand the value and cycle of the dollar. Therefore, schools should try to adopt and become a kind of "student-led credit union". Many people aren't aware that there are national programs that allow schools to function as credit unions. These schools organically teach students not only financial education, but the power of relationships and macroeconomics in the community, too. Creatively, we can get students' parents and non-profit organizations to donate to the student union to establish a network of cooperative economics for education and community empowerment. The capital you raise and the partnerships you develop with companies will then lead to...

- ## Employment/Industry

You've probably heard the saying, "Your students' network will impact their net worth." Therefore, if your school, as a community, really wants your students to be life-ready, you should work extremely hard to gather partnerships with businesses and organizations willing to employ your students. With a student led credit union and established partnership-building, the network of the school will continue to grow, which will increase the opportunities for students once they graduate, to have employers from the community that are willing to employ them, which increases the critical hope for students, which, in turn, improves the school's performance. You see how these items are building upon each other? Now that you have addressed the critical hope problem, we can address the...

- **Equality**

Now that the community and school have worked together to have a cycle of economics, education, and employment, the capital, along with the awareness of struggles, can be tackled. The community can start lobbying for a purposeful politician who is trusted by the community to support the movement for equality in the community. This ecosystem will then allow more people who are truly supportive of the community to be—more famously put by the Broadway hit, Hamilton—"in the room where it happens". This can only happen if the level of financial and social capital of the school and the community are collectively built. By establishing this, it gives the opportunity to make the changes needed to achieve the vision that all humans are created equal.

- **Equity**

Each community school will look different. For some schools to fully create an ecosystem of change, they will need huge donations from those who believe in the vision. To build a true "Community School", an equitable plan of sustainability will need to be established, and it will take district leaders and community leaders to challenge their current structures and comfort zones and truly come together to fight for real substantial change. Many high-performing schools are being replicated across the nation; however, the notion of replicating or scaling schools, in theory, may sound promising, but the DNA of each community varies, and you must take this into consideration as the work moves forward. Equity is not a one-size-fits-all concept. So if we are seeking deeper change, we must come with a deeper understanding of the challenges that our communities still face.

No matter how big or small your school is, you can transform it into the epicenter of your community's ecosystem. You can achieve this by making your school a place where students, parents, and families can work, grow, and play in healthy, productive ways. This is why you should value the principles like *collective work and responsibility* and *cooperative economics* because those principles will build the types of experiences that will grow a true community system. Your school doesn't stand on its own—it is part of your community. Therefore, you need to learn about your community's history, its leaders, and the present issues that it is facing so that you can do what's necessary to help out.

## A True Community School

*"The paradox of education is precisely this - that as one begins to become conscious, one begins to examine the society in which he is being educated."* (Baldwin).

The phrase "true community school" means that your school is more than the students who are enrolled in it. To become a true community school, you will do what is needed to create partnerships so that you can offer a range of opportunities and support to your students, families, youth, and communities. Revolutionizing your school to make it a community school involves the integration of academics, community and youth development, community engagement, social services, and health services. All of these will promote an improvement in your students' learning along with stronger families and communities.

If your school is empowered by your community, this means that you, your teachers, staff members, administrators, parents, students, and all the other members of the community feel that they are interested and involved in your school's success. An example of how you can encourage this is by asking parents and other volunteers to help in your classrooms. You can have special days when they will teach the students, or do other activities related to the current lessons being learned.

Your school can also benefit by receiving financial assistance and other forms of support from district personnel, corporations, local businesses, legislators, and non-profit agencies. If you remember my story about how Stix provided us with such support, which prompted others to do the same, this is one way your school can grow as part of the community. Creating a community school also involves a more personalized learning environment and curriculum that serves the community. Schools and districts that adopt a vision of all students achieving self-actualization will realize that in many cases, to reach this vision, schools should essentially be "community hubs" that are open practically 24 hours a day. You might think that something like this is radical, but it is possible. This framework will allow the school to provide education during regular school hours, and through a community-district partnership, the school will operate as a resource center the rest of the time. Imagine the resources that could be available for our youth. To provide this framework as essential resources, we will have to have a mindset of people and students before profits. To accomplish a community school, you can work together with partners to do the following:

- Be more than a school leader—become a community servant.

- Ensure that the community is welcome and represented throughout the school regularly.

- Encourage the BOOM effect in your students so that they take control of their community by learning the history and the why of their community so that they can make an impact.

- Plan activities that allow your students to engage in the community. Encourage parents and families to be involved with these activities, too.

- Encourage businesses, non-profits, churches, as well as parents and families to be involved with the education of your students.

In this type of environment, your students and their families have a wide range of support from your partners in the community. This will help your students realize that they live in a supportive, safe, and stable environment, which is ideal for learning. Your school and your community can leverage the human and physical assets that you share to ensure that your students will succeed in life.

## Offering Meaningful Opportunities to Participate

A healthy community needs a school they can rely on, and a healthy school also needs a stable community it can rely on. This means that your school and your community should work together to achieve greatness. One cannot be great without the other, so you should find ways to make things work for your benefit and the benefit of your community. "Successful" schools that solely get students out of their communities still leave communities in stagnation.

When it comes to involving your community in your revolution, you must offer them meaningful opportunities to participate. This shows that you value anyone who offers support and anyone who wants to get involved in your school—that you're not just trying to talk about it but you are trying to be about it. As per experience, here are some excellent examples of how you can provide meaningful opportunities to your community:

- **Offer workshops and classes to parents and community members**

Have you ever tried doing this? If not, you might be surprised at the amount of interest and support you will receive from the parents of your students and the other members of your community. To really make this powerful, request or recruit parents who can sometimes lead the workshops. I have found that parents listening and learning from other parents have been really successful. The fact is, parents want to support their children at home, especially in terms of academics. But the problem is, they seldom know how to do this. Therefore, offering workshops and classes to those who are interested is a meaningful way to involve them in your school's activities.

- **Involve the parents of your students as community organizers**

After the parents have learned a couple of things through your workshops and classes, ask them if they want to become community organizers too. Involve them in planning community events and ask them if they would like to host these with you. This isn't just meaningful, it will also help ease your burden as you enlist the help of those who want to provide it.

- **Host events that celebrate the successes of your students and community**

You should do this regularly, but add this subtle twist to some of your awards—during any ceremonies, create awards named after people or organizations to provide to your students. This will not only make the community feel truly part of the school, but it will make the student understand the value of community. Do this especially if you want people to take notice. During your celebratory event, invite parents and other members of the community, too. Such events will showcase your school, the achievements of your students, and give interested parties reasons for why they should support you.

When it comes to providing meaningful opportunities, you must think of these carefully. After all, you want to gain their trust, while inspiring them to join your school community. Other examples of how you can do this include:

- Inviting parents and other members of the community to be active co-creators of your school's programs, practices, and policies.

- Involving your community partners in the support of your students and their families. Do this by inspiring them with your school's message and showing them the benefits of being part of your school community.

- Inviting parents, business leaders, civic leaders, and funders to be members of your school's council.

- Encouraging your school's most avid supporters to become community leaders and advocates.

All these strategies and the ones you and your team come up with will help make your efforts more meaningful as you work to build your school community. Ask yourself this, how has my school maximized community partnerships?

## Raising Capital

In order for you to implement all of the plans you made, you need to have enough money or capital. Realistically speaking, money is an important part of running your school, so you must put time and effort into your fundraising efforts. Remember the obstacles we had discussed in Chapter 3? One of the most significant obstacles is the lack of resources. Although there are things you can do to overcome this obstacle, if you can find ways to raise money, you can make things easier for yourself.

Let's consider private schools for a moment. Often, school leaders of private schools don't have to deal with lacking resources because they have endowments. An endowment is a collection of assets from investments that are meant to support the mission of a school. Leaders of private schools use these endowments to support their students, and upgrades for their schools and their communities. With endowments, schools can make plans for the future since they know that they will always have the resources to achieve those plans.

Endowments are reliable, long-term financial supports that enable schools to increase student support, make commitments for their teachers and staff, develop programs for their teachers, initiate research, invest in technology, and maintain their facilities and physical assets. But what if you don't have endowments to rely on?

What then?

Although it will take more effort from you and your team, you must find ways to get funds for your school. Brainstorm with your team to come up with the most appropriate and interesting ideas to gain funds. You can also try reaching out to key people through social media, like the IG message I sent to Stix, which caused a ripple-effect that helped our school in so many ways.

However, you shouldn't rely on just one person or entity to support you. Personally, I believe that if you grant them permission to feed you, then you also give them permission to starve you. No matter how powerful a financier is, you should still make sure that you are in control. The financial support you receive should only be support. At the end of the day, you should still have the power and right to control your school's decisions. That way, you can always make sure that the decisions you make will always be beneficial to your school and community.

## Economic Strategies for a Self-Sufficient School

Money is an important part of running a school. While you can get financial support from powerful people, it would be better for you in the long run if you can find ways to make your school self-sufficient. For this, I have a number of economic action steps you may want to consider taking:

- Focus on your school's branding. Since you own this branding, you can choose to manage it however you wish. Highlight the best parts of your school, including its mission, vision, mantra, and core values. Take all of these into consideration to showcase your school's community power.

- Think of ways to create a self-sufficient community economy within your school. Some examples are PTA fundraising activities and non-profit organizations.

- Take aggressive (but appropriate) steps to attract talents and partnerships from communities, corporations, and schools all across the country.

- Focus on building your school's wealth by sharing your economic plans. You may also want to create a vertical vision model using macroeconomics as your basis.

- Amass a "mission and vision" capital for your school through community-based fundraising efforts. One way to do this is by promoting your school community's competitive advantages.

As you try these strategies, it's also a good idea to create "Safe Business Zones" so that all of the businesses and entities that choose to support you will follow a code of conduct. This will help prevent conflicts, which can affect your school community negatively.

# Take Time to Reflect

Have you ever thought about what the 4.0 student that continues the cycle of oppression does for your community?

As important as grades are, these shouldn't be your sole focus if you want to create a school that contributes positively to your community. Let me share an example with you of how one country that people seldom associate with great education—Paraguay—is providing economically empowering education for their youth. Paraguay has come up with a new and innovative model of vocational and technical education that is completely market-based. Educational opportunities are offered to their students by schools that are financially self-sufficient. They also provide all of their graduates with the opportunity to either continue with their education, find good jobs, or create their own employment. As you reflect on this, try to think of your answers to these questions too:

- How does your school impact the community?

- How can your school and community work together to improve the lives of the families in the community?

- How can financial support for your school and community become more sustainable?

# Conclusion:
# It's Time to Revolutionize

It's time for you to start your revolution. Now that you have reached the end of our learning journey, it's time for you to take action and become that revolutionary educator. As I had promised at the beginning of this book, I have shared with you the concepts, stories, and strategies that will help you start your own educational revolution in your school.

In the first chapter, we started by differentiating evolution from revolution. Evolution is something that comes gradually, and you don't need to do anything to make it happen. On the other hand, revolution is something that brings about incredible change—and this is what you want to achieve. In the same chapter, I shared with you the current situation of education. Right now, our educational system isn't ideal. Students of color always seem to be at a disadvantage, while white students get most of the privileges and opportunities. That is the reality that you want to change.

In Chapter 2, you learned everything about revolutionary leadership. By becoming an effective leader, you can start the revolution for which you are aiming. Of course, this is a process that will take time. If you start applying the things you have learned in this chapter, you will be well on your way to becoming the leader you need to be for your school. Before moving on to the principles of an educational revolution, we discussed the challenges of the educational system that you would have to deal with in Chapter 3. The obstacles we discussed here are the most significant ones that you would have to overcome. If you can do this, your journey will become much easier.

Chapter 4 is where you learned about organizational culture. Your school's culture is very important for everyone in your school, which is why you should try to nurture a positive culture. In this chapter, we defined what culture is and made the distinction between a positive and negative one. Then, you learned how to shape your school's organizational culture as part of your revolution. In Chapter 5, we started with the different principles of educational revolution: Setting the Stage, Revolutionizing Staff Performance, Restorative Practices, Revolutionizing Your School Culture (using traditional methods), Revolutionizing Your School Culture Using Social Media and Technology, Revolutionizing Your Data-Centered Culture, Revolutionizing Teaching and Learning, and Revolutionizing Your Community.

From start to finish, you have learned a wealth of information to help you make a real change. Remember that a revolution won't happen unless someone is brave enough to make it happen— as a leader, you must be that person. Now that you have all the knowledge and tools you need for your revolution, it's time for you to take action. With everything you have learned here, I would like to challenge you as the principal, or the head of your school, to continue teaching. Right now, I still teach a leadership class in my school even though I am the principal. My class is called "Young Kings", and each year, I teach 30 "at-hope" kings at my school. My aim is to transform all at-risk students to at-hope kings by teaching valuable lessons to them. I encourage the practice of continuing to teach a class, even as a leader, to keep you grounded and help you understand what your teachers are doing. This is another revolutionary change you should start in your school.

There is no time like the present to start making changes in your school. Soon, you will see how these changes are pushing your school to greatness. Before wrapping up this book, I would like to thank you for choosing to take your revolutionary learning journey with me. If you feel like you have learned what you needed in this book, I would really appreciate it if you would leave a review on Amazon for other aspiring revolutionary leaders to see. Now, you can go start your revolution with my last piece of advice: "Change the world, don't let the world change you."

# Acknowledgments

To my wife, Danielle: They say beside every great man is a greater woman. You embody that statement. Thank you for being the key that unlocked my hidden treasure as a man. Thank you for never letting me settle when it comes to my dreams. And thank you for being the most amazing mother and wife to our family.

To my daughter, Journee, "My Jalapeno": Thank you for allowing "Paddy" a.k.a. Daddy to spread his wings and fly. Thank you for understanding the phone calls and emails during playtime. I hope that one day you can forgive me as you work hard for your dreams.

To my parents, Abwakiya and Amen. Thank you for making me the man I am today. The lectures, the talks, the love I think paid off. I know you had your doubts plenty of times. But I hope I have made you both proud. Mom, thank you for being in my corner and being my #1 cheerleader. Pops, thank you for providing me with the sacred knowledge to be able to walk in my purpose.

To my Village: Y'all already know who you are and how we do it! Thank you for elevating my voice and supporting me through the peaks and the valleys. Thank you for pushing me to limits I never thought I could reach. Thanks for being my voice, when I felt voiceless, thank you for being my help, when I felt helpless, and thank you for being my hope when I felt hopeless.

# Speaking

Besides being a Revolutionary Educator and Principal, Amen Rahh revolutionizes the professional development experience for districts and schools across the nation. You can find him delivering keynotes at graduations and presenting workshops. As a founding Principal, Rahh's authenticity as a leader has him traveling across the world internationally to speak to educators who are seeking to revolutionize the educational experience.

Some of his most popular seminars focus on:

- Building a Restorative School Community: Restorative Justice

- Overcoming Systemic Racism in the Classroom and at the School

- Building an Aspirational Classroom and School Environment

- School Branding: The 10 Keys to Landing a Corporate Sponsor

- Trauma Informed Practices

- The 6 Keys to Unlocking Your School's Hidden Treasure

Amen Rahh provides resources and content at www.revolutionaryeducator.com. He can also be found on social media at @principalrahh. There, he shares more free resources and provides free workshops every Sunday and invites others to learn and grow with him toward becoming a Revolutionary Educator.

# References

Adams, J. Q. (2018). *PassItOn*. PassItOn. https://www.passiton.com/
inspirational-quotes/6728-if-your-actions-inspire-others-to-
dream-more

Amato, N. (2015). *A lack of resources for many classrooms*. New York
Times. https://www.nytimes.com/roomfordebate/2015/03/26/
is-im-proving-schools-all-about-money/a-lack-of-resources-for-
many-classrooms

American Civil Liberties Union. (2019). *School-to-Prison pipeline*.
American Civil Liberties Union. https://www.aclu.org/issues/
juvenile-justice/school-prison-pipeline

American Council on Education. (2014). *Understanding college and
university endowments*. American Council of Education. https://
www.acen-et.edu/Documents/Understanding-Endowments-
White-Paper. pdf

American Psychological Association. (2017, July). *Ethnic and
Racial Minorities & Socioeconomic Status*. American Psychological
Association. https://www.apa.org/pi/ses/resources/
publications/minorities

American University. (2018, July 11). *What the U.S. education system
needs to reduce inequality*. School of Education - American
University. https://soeonline.american.edu/blog/reducing-
inequality-in-the-us-education-system

Anyon, Y. (2017). *School-Wide restorative practices: Step by step.* Education Votes. http://educationvotes.nea.org/wp-content/uploads/2017/09/Implementation-Guide-2017-FINAL.pdfBeck, J. (2014, January 22). *Tips for teaching with limited classroom resources.* Go Overseas. https://www.gooverseas.com/blog/tips-for-teaching-with-limited-classroom-resources

Berkowitz, K. (n.d.). *Restorative practices whole-school implementation guide.* San Francisco Unified School District. https://www.healthiersf.org/RestorativePractices/Resources/documents/SFUSD%20Whole%20School%20Implementation%20Guide%20final.pdf

Blue Apple Education. (2016, December 13). *Boost your school's online presence.* Blue Apple Education. https://www.blueappleeducation.com/boost-your-schools-online-presence/

Burke, M. A., & Picus, L. O. (2001). *Developing community-empowered schools.* ERIC. Corwin Press, Inc. https://eric.ed.gov/?id=ED454621

Burstein, R. (2019, May 20). *The greatest barrier for educators changing their practice? Internal resistance.* EdSurge. https://www.edsurge.com/news/2019-05-20-the-greatest-barrier-for-educators-changing-their-practice-internal-resistance

Burt, M. (2017a). *The financially self-sufficient school: Education that pays for itself.* Changemakers. https://www.changemakers.com/socialbusiness/entries/financially-self-sufficient-school-education-pays

Burt, M. (2017b). *The financially self-sufficient school model – Paraguay: Economically empowering education for low-income youth.* Changemakers. https://www.changemakers.com/economicopportunity/entries/new-entry-105

Camp, J. (2015). *2.2 Poverty and race: How do students' backgrounds affect their school performance?* ED100. https://ed100.org/lessons/poverty

Carnegie Mellon University. (2020, February 11). *Revolutionizing education*. Carnegie Mellon University. https://www.cmu.edu/news/stories/archives/2020/february/open-simon.html

Centers for School Change. (2012, September 3). *Vision and mission*. Center for School Change. https://centerforschoolchange.org/publications/minnesota-charter-school-handbook/vision-and-mission/

Coalition for Community Schools. (2017). *What is a community school?* Community Schools. http://www.communityschools.org/aboutschools/what_is_a_community_school.aspx

Colannino, A. (2018, October 19). *Why school principals should learn every student's name*. HMHCO. https://www.hmhco.com/blog/why-school-principals-should-learn-every-students-name

Cole, J. (2018, April 20). *BRACKETS*. Genius. https://genius.com/J-cole-brackets-lyrics

Collins, J. (2017). *Clock building, not time telling*. Jim Collins. https://www.jimcollins.com/media_topics/Clock-Building.html

Cooper, J. (2016, August 4). *5 easy ways to grow your school social media following*. Campus Suite. https://www.campussuite.com/blog/5-easy-ways-to-grow-your-school-social-media-following

Couros, G. (2018, May 18). *Rita pierson – The principal of change*. George Couros. https://georgecouros.ca/blog/archives/tag/rita-pierson

Craig, W. (2018, May 15). *The importance of having a mission-driven company*. Forbes. https://www.forbes.com/sites/william-craig/2018/05/15/the-importance-of-having-a-mission-driven-company/#4b074b573a9c

Dash, A. (2016, November 11). *Lack of communication between teachers and students*. Toppr Bytes. https://www.toppr.com/bytes/failure-communication-between-teachers-and-students/Davis, A. (n.d.). *The freedom archives*. The Freedom Archives.

https://www.freedomarchives.org/audio_samples/Angela_Davis.html

Definition & Analysis of Institutional Racism. (n.d.). *Racial equality tools.* https://www.racialequitytools.org/resourcefiles/institutional-racism.pdf

Department of Education. (n.d.). *Collecting internal school data.* NSW Government. https://education.nsw.gov.au/teaching-and-learning/school-excellence-and-accountability/sef-evidence-guide/guidelines-for-using-data/collecting-internal-school-data

DeWitt, P. (2011, September 6). *Creating an inclusive school culture.* Education Week. https://blogs.edweek.org/edweek/finding_common_ground/2011/09/creating_an_inclusive_school_culture.html

Dinant, van. (2016, April 25). *Education needs a humanistic approach.* Trenducation. https://trenducation.wordpress.com/2016/04/25/education-needs-a-humanistic-approach/

Douglas, E. (2012, April 30). *Organizational structures and organizational change.* Education Week. https://blogs.edweek.org/topschool-jobs/k-12_talent_manager/2012/04/organizational_structures_and_organizational_change.html

Drew, C. (2019, June 18). *What is the humanistic theory in education? (2019).* The Helpful Professor. https://helpfulprofessor.com/humanist-theory-in-education/

Earp, J. (2016, March 21). *Overcoming obstacles to education delivery.* Teacher Magazine. https://www.teachermagazine.com.au/articles/overcoming-obstacles-to-education-deliver

EB. (2013, August 16). *Creating an online presence.* Education Business. https://educationbusinessuk.net/features/creating-online-presence

Education World. (2016). *Is your school's culture toxic or positive?* Education World. https://www.educationworld.com/a_admin/admin/admin275.shtml

Emerson, B. (2016). Introducing a holistic curriculum. *Antioch University.* https://www.antioch.edu/los-angeles/wp-content/uploads/sites/2/2016/12/A-Look-at-the-Current-Educational-System-Introducing-a-Holistic-Curriculum.pdf

Equinox Parent School Council. (n.d.). *The holistic curriculum.* Equinox Holistic Alternative School Parent Council. https://equinox-school.ca/about/the-holistic-curriculum/

Firdaus, F. A., & Mariyat, A. (2017, December). *Humanistic approach in education according to Paulo Freire.* Research Gate. https://www.researchgate.net/publication/322934319_Humanistic_Approach_In_Education_According_To_Paulo_Freire

Fordham University. (2020). *Conducting an environmental scan.* Fordham. https://www.fordham.edu/info/26625/conducting_an_environmental_scan

Fuller, R. B. (2013). *Richard Buckminster "Bucky" Fuller quotes.* Goodreads. https://www.wallacefoundation.org/knowledge-center/Documents/The-School-Principal-as-Leader-Guiding-Schools-to-Better-Teaching-and-Learning-2nd-Ed.pdf

Gabriel, J. G., & Farmer, P. C. (2009a). *Developing a vision and a mission.* ASCD. http://www.ascd.org/publications/books/107042/chapters/developing-a-vision-and-a-mission.aspx

Gabriel, J. G., & Farmer, P. C. (2009b). *How to help your school thrive without breaking the bank.* ASCD. http://www.ascd.org/publications/books/107042/chapters/Honing-Your-Leadership-and-Growing-New-Leaders.aspx

García, E., & Weiss, E. (2017, September 27). *Education inequalities at the school starting gate.* Economic Policy Institute. https://www.epi.org/publication/education-inequalities-at-the-school-starting-gate/

Glantz, A., & Martinez, E. (2018, February 15). *For people of color, banks are shutting the door to homeownership.*

Reveal. https://www.reveal-news.org/article/for-people-of-color-banks-are-shutting-the-door-to-homeownership/

Gradelink Representative. (2016, April 19). *How to effectively market your school: Your online presence.* Gradelink. https://www.gradelink.com/blog/how-to-effectively-market-your-school-part-2-building-online-presence/

Gray, L., Lewis, L., & Ralph, J. (2015). Public School Safety and Discipline: 2013 –14. In *National Center for Education Statistics* (pp. 1–55). https://nces.ed.gov/

Great Schools Partnership. (2013, November 25). *School culture definition.* The Glossary of Education Reform. https://www.edglossary.org/school-culture/

Groscurth, C. (2014, March 6). *Why your company must be mission-driven.* Gallup. https://www.gallup.com/workplace/236537/why-company-mission-driven.aspx

Gruenert, S., & Whitaker, T. (2015). *Defining organizational culture.* ASCD. http://www.ascd.org/publications/books/115004/chapters/Defining-Organizational-Culture.asp

Hallman, L. (2020, April 27). *Maslow before bloom: Educators need to meet learners' basic needs in time of pandemic.* Salzburg Global. https://www.salzburgglobal.org/news/latest-news/article/maslow-before-bloom-educators-need-to-meet-learners-basic-needs-in-time-of-pandemic

Harris, A. (2014, September 29). *Distributed leadership.* Teacher Magazine. https://www.teachermagazine.com.au/articles/distributed-leadership

Harris, D. A. (2020, January 21). *Racial profiling: Past, present, and future?* American Bar Association. https://www.americanbar.org/groups/criminal_justice/publications/criminal-justice-magazine/2020/winter/racial-profiling-past-present-and-future/

Heath, D. (n.d.). *Dan heath quote*. Quote Fancy. https://quotefancy. com/quote/1716228/Dan-Heath-Data-are-just-summaries-of-thousands-of-stories-tell-a-few-of-those-stories-to

Hesinger, M. (2018, January 30). *What if every school had a community ecosystem?* The Ecology Center. https://www.theecologycenter. org/what-if-every-school-had-a-community-ecosystem/

Hogan, J. (2018, March 31). *We must Maslow before we Bloom*. The Compelled Educator. http://www.thecompelleddeducator. com/2018/03/we-must-maslow-before-we-bloom.html

Houston, P. D. (n.d.). Using Data to Improve Schools Using Data to Improve Schools. In *AASA* (pp. 1–70). https:// aasa.org/uploadedFiles/Policy_and_Advocacy/files/ UsingDataToImprove-Schools.pdf

*How systemic racism infiltrates education*. (2017). Ben & Jerry. https:// www.benjerry.com/whats-new/2017/11/systemic-racism-education

iQerel. (n.d.). *School organisational culture*. Evaluation Plus. http://www. evaluationplus.eu/school-organisational-culture

Jarrett, K. (2016, March 10). *Middle school maker journey: The making of a mantra*. Edutopia. https://www.edutopia.org/blog/making-makerspace-care-think-design-act-kevin-jarrett

Jenkins, L. (2018, August 1). *4 reflections from a classroom teacher on restorative practices*. Mrs. Js Classroom. https://geochat.edublogs. org/2018/08/01/4-reflections-from-a-classroom-teacher-on-restorative-justice/

King University. (2018, April 20). *Equality vs. equity: A crucial difference in pedagogy*. King University Online. https://online.king.edu/ news/equality-vs-equity/

Lanier, J. T. (1997, July). *Redefining the role of the teacher: It's a multifaceted profession*. Edutopia. https://www.edutopia.org/redefining-role-teacher

Le Guin, U. K. (1974). *A quote from the dispossessed.* Goodreads. https://www.goodreads.com/quotes/221883-you-cannot-buy-the-revolution-you-cannot-make-the-revolution

Madylus, O. (2015, March 1). *Article 2 : How to deal with insufficient resources at school?* Share It, Don't Store It! https://eltdpshare.wordpress.com/videos-and-articles/article-2-how-to-deal-with-insufficient-resources-at-school/

Malaure, O. (2017, April 26). *Spring cleaning: Improve your school's online presence in 4 easy steps.* Finalsite. https://www.finalsite.com/blog/p/~board/b/post/spring-cleaning-improve-your-schools-online-presence-in-4-easy-steps

Malcolm X. (n.d.). *Malcolm X quote.* Quotefancy. https://quotefancy.com/quote/859209/Malcolm-X-We-can-t-teach-what-we-dont-know-and-we-can-t-lead-where-we-can-t-go

McGraw-Hill. (2018, October 24). *What's the difference between equity and equality in education?* Medium. https://medium.com/inspired-ideas-prek-12/whats-the-difference-between-equity-and-equality-in-education-ef20971e7fda

Meador, D. (2019). *Common school issues that negatively impact learning.* ThoughtCo. https://www.thoughtco.com/issues-that-negatively-impacts-student-learning-3194421

Mullen, G. (2020, April 2). *"Maslow before Bloom."* Exploring the Core. https://www.exploringthecore.com/post/maslow-before-bloom

NCES. (2018). *Public high school graduation rates.* National Center for Education Statistics. https://nces.ed.gov/programs/coe/indicator_coi.asp

Nelson, L., & Lind, D. (2015, February 24). *The school to prison pipeline, explained.* Justice Policy. http://www.justicepolicy.org/news/8775

Newman, P. (2019, June 19). *How to integrate restorative practices, justice & discipline with PBIS*. Kickboard. https://www.kickboardforschools. com/restorative-practices-justice/how-to-integrate-restor-ative-practices-justice-discipline-with-pbis/

Norton. (2008). Chapter 7: The staff development and performance evaluation processes. *Sage Pub*. https://www.sagepub.com/sites/ default/files/upm-binaries/21423_Chapter_7.pdf

Oppmann, A.-K. (n.d.). *Creating a data-driven culture*. BI Survey. https://bi-survey.com/data-driven-culture#recom

Pattonville School-Community Relations. (n.d.). A principal's top 10 list for successful communications. *NSPRA* (pp. 1–2). https:// www.nspra.org/files/PrincipalsTop10.pdf

PBIS. (2010). *Tier 2*. PBIS. https://www.pbis.org/pbis/tier-2

PBIS. (2019a). *Home Page*. PBIS. https://www.pbis.org/

PBIS. (2019b). *Tier 1*. PBIS. https://www.pbis.org/pbis/tier-1

PBIS. (2019c). *Tier 3*. PBIS. https://www.pbis.org/pbis/tier-3

Poole, M. L. (1991). Environmental scanning is vital to strategic planning. In *ASCD* (pp. 1–3). http://www.ascd.org/ASCD/pdf/ journals/ed_lead/el_199104_poole.pdf

Prithviraj. (2017, December 26). *Revolutionizing education*. IndianFolk. https://www.indianfolk.com/revolutionizing-education/

Queen Rania of Jordan. (n.d.). *Queen rania of jordan quotes*. Brainy Quote. https://www.brainyquote.com/quotes/queen_rania_of_ jordan_571460

Reform Support Network. (2014). Strategies for community engagement in school turnaround. *US Department of Education* (pp. 1–24).

https://www2.ed.gov/about/inits/ed/implementation-support-unit/tech-assist/strategies-for-community-engagement-in-school-turnaround.pdf

Reid, C. (2018, September 12). *7 tips for facilitating communication between teachers, administrators, and parents.* Jotform Blog. https://www.jotform.com/blog/7-tips-for-facilitating-communication-between-teachers-administrators-and-parents/

Relojo-Howell, D. (2019, January 19). *How can social media help education?*

Psychreg. https://www.psychreg.org/social-media-education/

Richardson, I. (2018, November 6). *The benefits of social media in school - Insights and expert advice.* Schudio. https://www.schudio.com/the-benefits-of-using-social-media-in-schools/

Riley, E. (2017, March 17). *Implementing restorative practices in the classroom.* Getting Smart. https://www.gettingsmart.com/2017/03/imple-menting-restorative-practices-in-the-classroom/

Robbins, B., Vincent, S., Middle, W., & Poland, S. (2018). restorative practices in action. *School Counselor.* https://www.schoolcounselor.org/asca/media/PDFs/WebinarPowerPoints/7-15-18_11-12_RobbinsVincent_RestorativePractices.pdf

Ryerse, M. (2017, January 17). *5 reasons self-awareness matters for leaders.* Getting Smart. https://www.gettingsmart.com/2017/01/5-reasons-self-awareness-matters-leaders/

Salvaire, A. (2013, July 1). *The education revolution.* The A Factor. https://www.theafactor.org/the-education-revolution/

Sauter, M. B. (2018, October 10). *Faces of poverty: What racial, social groups are more likely to experience it?* USA TODAY. https://www.usato-day.com/story/money/economy/2018/10/10/faces-poverty-social-racial-factors/37977173/

Scott King, C. (n.d.). *Coretta scott king quotes.* Brainy Quote. https://www.brainyquote.com/quotes/coretta_scott_king_810146

Sellberg, E. (2018, May 4). *Incorporating the 5 love languages in the workplace.* Medium. https://medium.com/@esellberg22/incorporating-the-5-love-languages-in-the-workplace-ba0ab9eb982

Shakur, T. (n.d.). *A quote by tupac shakur.* Goodreads. https://www.goodreads.com/quotes/135997-i-m-not-saying-i-m-gonna-change-the-world-but-i

Shaw, A. (n.d.). *Obstacles to overcome.* 21st Century Schools. https://www.21stcenturyschools.com/obstacles.html

Sheninger, E. (2019, May 26). *A principal's reflections: The challenges educators face.* A Principal's Reflections. http://esheninger.blogspot.com/2019/05/the-challenges-educators-face.html

Shores, K., Kim, H. E., & Still, M. (2020, February 21). *Categorical inequal-ities between black and white students are common in US schools—But they don't have to be.* Brookings. https://www.brookings.edu/blog/brown-center-chalkboard/2020/02/21/categorical-inequalities-between-black-and-white-students-are-common-in-us-schools-but-they-dont-have-to-be/

Siegel, E. (2020). *Seven key metrics for tracking student success.* Campus Intelligence. https://www.campusintelligence.com/2019/04/30/seven-key-metrics-for-tracking-student-success/

Silver, A. (2019, April 14). *Building clocks: The mindset for operational autonomy.* Medium. https://medium.com/@amsilverny/building-clocks-the-mindset-for-operational-autonomy-198954c4394e

Snow, S. (2012, August 9). *Repeat after me: Your company needs a mantra.* Fast Company. https://www.fastcompany.com/3000236/repeat-after-me-your-company-needs-mantra

Solaun, M. (2020). *A bad principal taught me a good lesson.* Scholastic. https://www.scholastic.com/teachers/articles/teaching-content/bad-principal-taught-me-good-lesson/

State Education Resource Center. (n.d.). *Embedding restorative practices within a PBIS framework to support student success.* SERC. https://ctserc.org/news/2015/embedding-restorative-practices-with-in-a-pbis-framework-to-support-student-success

Stevenson, B. (2019, August 14). *Why american prisons owe their cruelty to slavery.* The New York Times. https://www.nytimes.com/interactive/2019/08/14/magazine/prison-industrial-complex-slavery-racism.html

*Strategies for developing core values at your school.* (2018, October 24). Catapult Learning. https://catapultlearning.com/2018/10/24/strategies-for-developing-core-values-at-your-school/

The Western States Center. *A history: the construction of race and racism.* https://www.racialequitytools.org/resourcefiles/Western%20States%20-%20Construction%20of%20Race.pdf

Stribbell, H. (2014, November 14). *Engaging your school community through social media.* Edutopia. https://www.edutopia.org/blog/engaging-school-community-social-media-howard-stribbell

Teasley, M. L. (2016). Organizational culture and schools: A call for leadership and collaboration. *Children & Schools, 39*(1), 3–6. https://doi.org/10.1093/cs/cdw048

*The four disciplines of organizational health.* (n.d.). Leadership Now. https://www.leadershipnow.com/leadingblog/2012/03/the_four_disciplines_of_organi.html

The New School. (2020, June 11). *Community and education during a global pandemic.* The New School. https://www.thenewschool.org/

about/news-blog/p/~board/p/post/community-and-education-during-a-global-pandemic

The Wallace Foundation. (2013). *The school principal as leader: Guiding schools to better teaching and learning.* The Wallace Foundation. https://www.wallacefoundation.org/knowledge-center/Documents/The-School-Principal-as-Leader-Guiding-Schools-to-Better-Teaching-and-Learning-2nd-Ed.pdf

Toch, T. (2017, June 27). *How D.C. schools are revolutionizing teaching.* Education Next. https://www.educationnext.org/d-c-schools-revolutionizing-teaching/

Traylor, D. (2019, September 20). *Incompetency on display: The unfortunate stories of bad school administrators.* Owlcation. https://owlcation.com/academia/Incompetency-on-Display-the-Unfortunate-Stories-of-Bad-School-Administrators

UNESCO. (2018, June 7). *#YouthOfUNESCO: Revolutionizing education!* UNESCO. https://en.unesco.org/news/youthofunesco-revolutionizing-education

U.S. Department of Education Office for Civil Rights. (2014). Civil rights data collection data Snapshot: School discipline. *Civil Rights Data Collection* (pp. 1–24). https://ocrdata.ed.gov/

Valant, J. (2020, June 4). *The banality of racism in education.* Brookings. https://www.brookings.edu/blog/brown-center-chalkboard/2020/06/04/the-banality-of-racism-in-education/

Waller, D. (2020, February 6). *10 steps to creating a data-driven culture.* Harvard Business Review. https://hbr.org/2020/02/10-steps-to-creating-a-data-driven-culture

Walsh, B. S. (n.d.). *If you don't know where you are going, how can you expect to get there?* Quotes. https://www.quotes.net/quote/18719

Walter, E. (2014, September 24). *Mantras that guide thriving organizations.* Forbes.https://www.forbes.com/sites/ekaterinawalter/2014/09/24/mantras-that-guide-thriving-organizations/#10e5c291429c

Watt, N., & Hannah, J. (2020, February 15). *Racist language is still woven into home deeds across america. Erasing it isn't easy, and some don't want to.* CNN. https://edition.cnn.com/2020/02/15/us/racist-deeds-covenants/index.html

Weir, K. (2016, November). Inequality at school. *American Psychological Association.* https://www.apa.org/monitor/2016/11/cover-in-equality-school

*Why understanding equity vs equality in schools can help you create an inclusive classroom.* (2019, May 2). Waterford.Org. https://www.waterford.org/education/equity-vs-equality-in-education/

Willis, O. (2016, October 11). *3 steps to organize student data—And find joy.* EdSurge. https://www.edsurge.com/news/2016-10-11-3-steps-to-organize-student-data-and-find-joy

Winter, R. (2012, April 12). *Case study: What does it take to turn around a school?* Edutopia. https://www.edutopia.org/blog/turn-around-school-rick-winter

CPSIA information can be obtained
at www.ICGtesting.com
Printed in the USA
BVHW050216290623
666555BV00007B/200